ENDORSEMENTS

With sound Biblical truth and through personal experiences, Rabbi breaks down the lies of the enemy and answers tough questions like "Why do bad things happen to good people?"

—DUSTIN

In a genuine and transparent way, Rabbi Schneider reveals the fears that tormented him - and may of us - through the years, bringing all to the foot of the cross and colorfully encouraging us all that we are not alone; God is with us and thus we can confront our fears by advancing toward them, not cowering in the shadows as soon-victims.

—ERIC SMITH, President, SMG

Someone has said, "The thing you concentrate on tends to increase." Rabbi Schneider has given us a beautiful picture of this experiential truth. Through his own personal journey, Rabbi put an end to fear in his life by concentrating on love—which "casts out fear." Through the indwelling Holy Spirit, Rabbi unpacks a simple truth that has plagued mankind down through the ages. This is a prescription for a vital forward moving Christianity. I highly recommend it.

—SCOTT KELSO, Chairman, Charismatic Leaders Fellowship

Rabbi's latest book is a much needed answer to all followers of Christ, and a much needed resource for the church.

—PASTOR EDWARD SMITH, Chaplain, TBN

ACKNOWLEDGMENTS

I would like to acknowledge and thank Father God, Yeshua/Jesus, and the Holy Spirit. I would also like to thank and acknowledge my wife Cynthia, for being His vessel of healing to me.

I would also like to thank my editors, Lloyd Hildebrand, Ryan Adair, and Terri Meckes for their patience and expertise.

For from Him and through Him and to Him are all things. To Him be the glory forever. Amen (Romans 11:36

DESTINY IMAGE BOOKS BY RABBI K. A. SCHNEIDER

Awakening to Messiah

DO NOT BE AFRAID!

HOW TO FIND
FREEDOM FROM FEAR

MESSIANIC RABBI
K. A. SCHNEIDER

DESTINY IMAGE® PUBLISHERS, INC.

P.O. Box 310, Shippensburg, PA 17257-0310

"Promoting Inspired Lives."

This book and all other Destiny Image, Revival Press, MercyPlace, Fresh Bread, Destiny Image Fiction, and Treasure House books are available at Christian bookstores and distributors worldwide.

For a U.S. bookstore nearest you, call 1-800-722-6774.

For more information on foreign distributors, call 717-532-3040.

Reach us on the Internet: www.destinyimage.com.

ISBN 13 TP: 978-0-7684-0402-9

ISBN 13 Ebook: 978-0-7684-0403-6

For Worldwide Distribution, Printed in the U.S.A.

2 3 4 5 6 7 8 / 18 17 16 15 14

CONTENTS

Editor's Note 9

Introduction. 11

CHAPTER 1   My Own Struggles. 17

CHAPTER 2   Jesus: The Way to Victory 27

CHAPTER 3   Fear: A Universal Problem 33

CHAPTER 4   Declaring War on Fear 41

CHAPTER 5   Knowing God Is with Us 53

CHAPTER 6   Dwelling Under the Shadow of the Most High. 63

CHAPTER 7   Applying God's Word 75

CHAPTER 8   God Is Bigger than Our Fear 85

CHAPTER 9   No Fear: Being Different from the World 95

CHAPTER 10   God's Greatest Desire 107

CHAPTER 11   Walking with God. 117

CHAPTER 12   The Power of the Holy Spirit. 133

CHAPTER 13   The Marvelous Grace of Our Loving Lord 139

CHAPTER 14   The Victorious Life 147

CHAPTER 15   So, Do You Really Want to Be Free? 157

EDITOR'S NOTE

The names Jesus and Yeshua (the Hebrew name for Jesus) are used interchangeably throughout this book in order to show that He is the Messiah of both Jews and Gentiles. This is in accordance with Paul's writings: *"For I am not ashamed of the gospel, for it is the power of God for salvation to everyone who believes, to the Jew first and also to the Greek"* (Rom. 1:16).

Rabbi Schneider has interwoven Bible-based prayers throughout the text as well. He hopes you will join in the spirit of these important prayers so you will be strengthened as you read. In doing so, you will engage the power of the Holy Spirit, and He will enable you to overcome your fears and find help in every area of your life.

INTRODUCTION

For God has not given us a spirit of timidity
[fear], *but of power and love and discipline*
[self-control] (2 Timothy 1:7).

WHY I WROTE THIS BOOK

Beloved, I know the torment that fear can bring. It is a real enemy that needs to be defeated in our lives, and I want you to learn how to be victorious over it in your own life. More importantly, I want you to find the freedom Jesus promises to you throughout the Scriptures: *"You will know the truth, and the truth will make you free"* (John 8:32).

Do Not Be Afraid: How to Find Freedom from Fear is more than just a book. My hope is that it is a powerful tool through which God will impart to you what is needed to become more than a conqueror in Christ Jesus (Rom. 8:31-39). His grace will be at work in your life as you read these pages, empowering you with new strength. I pray that you will find the way and the strength necessary to overcome fear. This is my goal and hope for you in writing this book. I know God wants this for all of His children.

As you read this unique book, I believe the Holy Spirit will give you a spiritual breakthrough so that you will be empowered to overcome fear. God loves us with an everlasting love, and His love is the perfect antidote for any fear we may face, for *"there is no fear in love; but perfect love casts out fear"* (1 John 4:18). As you experience the love of God in a fresh way and learn to trust Him with your heart, your fears will depart and be replaced by His presence.

BONDAGE TO FEAR

The reality is that everybody struggles with fear, just like I have throughout my life. I've struggled with fear since I was a child, but God in His great faithfulness has set me free from many things and is continuing to set me free. He will do the same for you too. *"So if the Son makes you free, you will be free indeed"* (John 8:32).

It is God's desire that His people live free from fear. As you read and meditate upon the truths of God's Word contained within, you will receive biblical revelation about the causes, effects, and solutions to fear. As you apply these truths through prayer and faith, you will discover a new freedom and will learn to walk in spiritual liberty—the liberty Christ purchased for every one of us through the cross.

Here is my prayer for you:

> *That the God of our Lord Jesus Christ, the Father of glory, may give to you a spirit of wisdom and of revelation in the knowledge of Him. I pray that the eyes of your heart may be enlightened, so that you will know what is the hope of His calling, what are the riches of the glory of His inheritance in the saints, and what is the surpassing greatness of His power toward us who believe* (Ephesians 1:17-19).

One of the Scriptures I refer to often in this book is Psalm 91. In this glorious chapter we learn that God is our refuge, our fortress, and our defender. He is also our protector, shield, and our place of safety. By knowing this about God, we are ready to wage war against every type of fear that tries to invade our hearts and lives.

I would encourage you now to read Psalm 91 and to consider the realities it proclaims as a helpful preparation for reading *Do Not Fear!*

He who dwells in the shelter of the Most High will abide in the shadow of the Almighty. I will say to the Lord, "My refuge and my fortress, my God, in whom I trust!" For it is He who delivers you from the snare of the trapper and from the deadly pestilence. He will cover you with His pinions, and under His wings you may seek refuge; His faithfulness is a shield and bulwark.

You will not be afraid of the terror by night, or of the arrow that flies by day; of the pestilence that stalks in darkness, or of the destruction that lays waste at noon. A thousand may fall at your side and ten thousand at your right hand, but it shall not approach you. You will only look on with your eyes and see the recompense of the wicked. For you have made the Lord, my refuge, even the Most High, your dwelling place. No evil will befall you, nor will any plague come near your tent.

For He will give His angels charge concerning you, to guard you in all your ways. They will bear you up in their hands, that you do not strike your foot against a stone. You will tread upon the lion and cobra, the young lion and the serpent you will trample down.

"Because he has loved Me, therefore I will deliver him; I will set him securely on high, because he has known My name. He will call upon Me, and I will answer him; I will be with him in trouble; I will rescue him and honor him. With a long life I will satisfy him and let him see My salvation" (Psalm 91).

MANY TYPES OF FEAR

In these times of social and economic upheaval, people are more afraid than ever. Many people have real fear when it comes to the possibility of running out of money, experiencing betrayal by a lover or friend, being fired from a job, or losing their home. In today's society where so many families are being torn apart and separated geographically, the fear of growing old and winding up in a nursing home alone plagues many. These are genuine fears that lead to great anxiety, worry, and even despair.

To make my point, consider this partial list of the many and varied fears and phobias people today are living with.

1. The fear of death.

2. The fear of getting sick.

3. The fear of running out of money.

4. The fear of being betrayed by a spouse or loved one.

5. The fear of being fired.

6. The fear of being in a hospital.

7. The fear of war.

8. The fear of public speaking.

9. The fear of car accidents.

10. The fear of something happening to a loved one.

Have you ever dealt with any of the phobias listed above, or any others for that matter? There are hundreds of different kinds of fears that people are grappling with on a daily basis—both ourselves, as well as people we come into contact with. Some of these fears totally immobilize while others make life very difficult at best.

Though some of these fears may seem common, and thus normal, the truth is that Satan is behind every phobia faced by humanity. Jesus says that Satan *"is a liar and the father of lies"* (John 8:44). We must learn to resist him—*"Be of sober spirit, be on the alert. Your adversary, the devil, prowls around like a roaring lion, seeking someone to devour. But resist him, firm in your faith, knowing that the same experiences of suffering are being accomplished by your brethren who are in the world"* (1 Pet. 5:8-9)—and I believe this book will help you to do this in effective and practical ways.

Lieutenant John B. Putnam Jr. once wrote, "Courage is not the lack of fear but the ability to face it."[1] We must stand up to and face our fears to find peace. When I was a little boy, I remember walking in our neighborhood, and a little boy named Dicky would throw rocks at me. I went home and told my dad, and he said, "You've got to stand up to him." The next time when Dicky started to throw rocks at me, I went up to him and hit him in the face. He never threw a rock at me again. In fact, we actually became friends after that.

It is my hope that this book will help you face fear and defeat it.

Prayer: *Abba Father, help me not to be afraid as I learn to dwell in Your secret place and to abide under the shadow of Your wings. You are my refuge and my fortress; I choose to trust in You. Because I believe Your Word, I will not fear. Through faith in Jesus my Messiah I will be an overcomer. Thank You, Father, for always being with me. In the name of Yeshua I pray, amen.*

ENDNOTE

1.   This quote was taken from http://www.phobialist.com/fears.html, accessed September 24, 2013.

I

MY OWN STRUGGLES

Have I not commanded you? Be strong and courageous!
Do not tremble or be dismayed, for the Lord your
God is with you wherever you go (Joshua 1:9).

THE NATURE OF FEAR

Fear is part of the human condition, and every person has dealt with it in different ways throughout their lives. I've dealt with fear throughout my own life, and I know that I'm not alone in this fight. Throughout this chapter I want to share with you many of the fears that I've had throughout my life. The lessons in this book come from my years of struggling against fear. God has delivered me from many fears, and He can do the same for you.

Fear is an instinctive emotion that is aroused by a perception of danger, either real or imagined, and causes anxiety and worry to arise within the human heart.

WRESTLING WITH FEAR

Prior to my acceptance of *Yeshua Hamashiach* as my Messiah, I wrestled with many irrational fears that seemed rational at the time. While I still battle with the devil on a daily basis, I am happy to report that my loving Father has given me great freedom and victory over fear in many areas of my life. This doesn't mean that I never experience fear at all, but I'm aware of it when it comes and have learned how to war against it and gain victory.

It is my desire that you will be able to identify with me and the challenges I've faced throughout my lifetime. And more importantly, as I share what I've learned, I believe that you will find hope and come to know that there is a way out. For Jesus promised us, *"If you continue in My word, then you are truly disciples of Mine; and you will know the truth, and the truth will make you free"* (John 8:31-32). In this book we will learn about the escape route God has provided for us when debilitating fear tries to stop us from fulfilling God's purposes in our lives.

Fears in the Night

As a Jewish boy growing up in Cleveland, Ohio, I knew very little about God and His ways. My parents were not very religious, but I was trained in Jewish culture and traditions. Most Jews are secular rather than religious, so for many of them being Jewish is a matter of culture rather than having an intimate personal relationship with God. This is the way my parents approached Judaism.[1]

I'm sure my parents did the best they knew how, but my father had come from a dysfunctional home in which he was treated much like an orphan. His parents were Jewish immigrants who came from Europe and barely spoke any English. He was often left alone while they went about peddling their goods. Although no home is perfect, I understood they loved me.

When I was a little boy, I was often afraid to go to sleep at night. I was certain that some monster would swing through my window like

Tarzan from a tree in the yard next door, grab me, and take me away, never to be seen again. I could picture these evil monsters in my mind's eye, and I was really scared. Their imagined presence would be reinforced in my mind as I lay in bed at night.

Those nightly experiences are the stuff of which horror movies are made. The truth is that I was living my own horror movie. I hated nighttime, for that was the time when monsters, ghosts, and other strange entities would appear in my imagination. More than just a fear of the dark, though, it was a fear of the unknown, of losing control, and of even dying. I was a scared little boy.

Fear of Losing Control

I remember a time when my family and I went for a cruise on a big boat. As we floated on the water, I had a panicky feeling that I would lose control and throw myself overboard. It took all my energy to fight this irrational fear. I had no reason to throw myself overboard, nor did I want to; but there was something within me causing me to be terrified that I would actually do something I didn't want to do. Both the boat and the water were frightening to me. It was an environment that felt so much bigger than me. I felt like I would lose control and hurl myself into the water. Experiences like these causes one to lose self-confidence and sense of identity.

Another fear of losing control arose when I started driving, especially when I was driving on unfamiliar highways. I feared I would lose control of myself, involuntarily take the wheel and drive the car into another car or the guardrail. I felt I would just lose control and end up dying.

The Fear of Poison

As I aged, prior to my *bar mitzvah* (at the age of thirteen), I battled with other fears, not the least of which was my paranoia about being poisoned. I was only eight years old when this fear took hold of me. In those days oral thermometers were filled with silver-colored mercury, which I knew to be extremely poisonous. Whenever someone took my temperature, I was afraid that they would drop the thermometer and break its glass, certain that the poisonous mercury would bounce from the shattered glass into my mouth, thereby killing me.

In a very real sense, my fear of poison was a fear of death. It may seem surprising to some that a boy of eight would fear death, but I certainly did. To me, death was the end of everything. Nothing that I learned in my Jewish training ever told me otherwise. As far as I knew, there was no after-life—life on this earth was it. To me, the idea of death was like going into a dark abyss that was filled with terror.

During this phase of my life, my school had a safety poster contest. We all designed posters to warn students of possible disasters and how to avoid them. Many of my fellow students developed posters that dealt with fire protection, safety on the sidewalks and streets, water safety, and the importance of not speaking to strangers, etc. Not me.

As you might suspect, my poster warned about the dangers of poison, and it was the only one that dealt with that particular topic. It was so different from the others'—theirs were so practical and dealt with things people encountered in their day-to-day lives. But I had a different point of view of what was practical. So I actually designed the poster with my own fears in mind.

It must have been that difference that enabled me to be one of the five winners of the school contest; it could not have been my artwork and penmanship, that's for sure. My prize was a transistor radio, which I treasured, but my intense fear about being poisoned still remained. Even though I was a happy child, darkness and fear still tormented me.

A Fear of Dying

At one point my fear of dying became almost overwhelming to me. For example, when I was eleven, I developed an obsessive-compulsive behavior that was related to this fear. Even though it was completely irrational, I became ritualistic in my belief that if I touched things with my left hand but did not touch them with my right hand (and vice versa), I would simply die. To be sure, it was a form of superstition, but at the time it tormented me.

This superstition reached its worst when my family and I drove from Cleveland, Ohio to Cape Cod, Massachusetts for a vacation on the ocean. The trip took two days traveling in the car, and all along the way my obsessive fear of touching things with both hands kept me very busy. There were a couple of times when I did not touch an item with both of my hands—I feared I would soon die.

I had no idea where my need to perform this strange ritual came from, but now I know that the devil was behind this. He wanted to paralyze me with fear. Praise God that after this trip the fear finally broke.

ADOLESCENCE: WRESTLING AND LOOKING FOR SIGNIFICANCE

Jewish boys have their bar mitzvah at the age of thirteen, which is considered to be the age of accountability. To prepare for this significant event, I attended Hebrew school three times a week, and there I learned about Jewish traditions, memorized prayers, and learned how to read Hebrew. But in spite of my bar mitzvah, I did not know anything about God. I believed in Him, but He was a distant figure.

During this time I began to see that the world was not a safe place. I would pick up a newspaper and read how somebody just got attacked, died in a car accident, or got cancer. It was also during this time that I realized that the authority figures and role models I once admired, people whom I thought had it all together, really didn't have it all together. When I discovered this, it was disturbing and led me to feel even less secure about my life and the world I lived in. I was becoming more aware of how unsafe the world was, and how things could happen to me that were outside of my control. These realities made me feel vulnerable, afraid, and insecure. All these thoughts and experiences combined to drive me to find an environment where I felt I was in control.

In seventh grade I decided to get involved with the sport of wrestling. One of my cousins was a wrestler and I greatly admired him. Though I was small for my age—and still am, for that matter—in wrestling I competed against people my own size. Wrestling began to form the core of my identity, the essence of who I was as I excelled in it.

As I look back on those years, I think wrestling was an activity that made me feel safe and secure and in charge of my situation because it gave me a measure of control over my environment—the wrestling mat.

My overriding thought during this time became, "I am going to become state champion." I lived it, ate it, slept it, and drank it. I was like a professional athlete training all year long. I thought that becoming state champ would set me up to live in victory for the rest of my life. Somehow, I believed that such an accomplishment would be all I would ever need to feel complete, to feel victorious and in control of everything. I was certain that no one in the state of Ohio trained more than I did for the title. I would listen to the song *Southern Man* by Crosby, Stills, and Nash every night and picture myself with my hands raised above my head as the state champion of Ohio in my weight class.

Without understanding it, I was looking for identity and security, something to validate me. Wrestling was a way of being affirmed both as a person and as a man. If I achieved the title of state champ, it would say to me, "You're the best." This was the kind of significance I was looking for, and it was a desperate need in my life.

FEAR PARALYZED ME

In tenth grade, I had the experience of losing a few wrestling matches because of my performance anxiety about winning. I would start out wrestling very aggressively, but once I got the lead, I would move into a mode of wrestling defensively out of fear of losing my lead. All of this culminated in twelfth grade when I lost a match that I should have easily won. Again, I was allowing fear to beat me, rather than my opponent. After this loss, I got so mad that I made up my mind to never let fear defeat me again. From that moment on I was determined to win, and I usually did. I felt I could beat anyone.

For the rest of my senior year, I lived on a high, winning matches and feeling like I was soaring in life. This ended very abruptly, however, when I walked off the wrestling mat after wrestling my last match in school. Suddenly I was consumed by fear, realizing that the world was a lot bigger than wrestling and people who wrestled my weight class. Life in high school was over, and I was now entering the real world.

It was such a big place. "What would I do now?" I thought to myself. My identity and purpose had been that of a 119-pound wrestler, and now it didn't mean anything anymore. My identity and purpose were gone. Who was I? Where was I going? Although I never won the state championship, I did receive a small wrestling scholarship to the University of Tampa, but it didn't mean anything because I realized that being a good wrestler was no longer relevant in the larger world.

Satan saw his opportunity and he moved in on me with a vengeance. I ended up going to a psychologist I had seen a couple of years before for career counseling and testing. His advice? "Your mind is just racing. What you need to do is go out and run." As you can imagine, running did not solve my problems. I ran nonetheless hoping it would help.

SEARCH FOR A FATHER

Without fully realizing it, I hungered for a father to be close with me and to learn from. As I said before, my dad did what he could, but my relationship with him was distant and sometimes cold. In the tenth grade I remember wanting my wrestling coach to put his arm around me and say, "Well done, son." I longed to have him call me "son."

I believe my father's lack of affirmation made me vulnerable to an attack from a homosexual demon. I had opened the door to spirits of lust through my use of pornography. My desire was for women, but one night a male demon (an incubus, which looked like a man with wings) sexually attacked me in my sleep. This was extremely unsettling because I considered myself to be thoroughly heterosexual, and I had a high commitment to manhood.

As a result of this demonic attack, I started questioning my sexuality. This doubting of my heterosexuality eventually eroded my masculine identity. I was tormented by the fear that I would turn into a homosexual, which would have meant the loss of my identity as a man. I had, and still do have, the highest commitment to manhood. To me, homosexuality and true manhood are incompatible with one another. If God had not set me free from this fear and deception, it would have completely destroyed me. This period of mental attack lasted for about two years, between the ages of eighteen and twenty.

SEARCH FOR SUCCESS

Although I was able to function as a college student, and my grades had been okay during this time, my loss of identity and purpose almost destroyed me. I spent a lot of time sleeping just to get away from the multitude of fears that constantly plagued me. As I contemplated my future, my fear and uncertainty increased and it was difficult to cope.

Many Jewish parents want their sons to become doctors or attorneys. Although I had always wanted to be doctor, I knew that I did not possess the necessary academic skills. I thought about becoming a lawyer because I had good communication skills that would be important, but then I wondered what I would do upon retirement: "Would I have to go through the same thing then that I was going through now? No future. No identity. No purpose."

I thought that perhaps becoming wealthy would help me to get free from the fear I was dealing with. But then I realized that even wealthy people had problems too. My life had no foundation, no focus, and no goals to strive after. I felt aimless, empty, and purposeless.

I attended the University of Tampa for a year and then dropped out with the thought in mind that I would open a discotheque. The year was 1978 and discos were really hot during the late seventies. In order to get the money to go into business, I began selling encyclopedias door to door.

Even though I encountered some success as a salesman and sales manager, I was still lost and searching. I began to read New Age literature, such as *Autobiography of a Yogi*. The fantastic feats and pictures of yogis levitating fascinated me. I wanted to pursue the ability to do these things, for I imagined that it would feel fantastic to be able to levitate off the ground. One summer night in 1978, however, the Lord put a stop to my blind searching and my wrong thinking.

Prayer: *Dear Father, I thank You for saving me and showing me Your ways. Help me to rise above all fear by trusting in Your Word, which tells me that You are always with me. Thank You for revealing Yeshua Hamashiach to me. Help me to cling to Him in faith and love. I love You, Father, and through Your grace, I will obey You. I will walk in faith, and I will trust in You without leaning upon my own understanding. In all my ways I will acknowledge You, and I know You will direct my steps. Thank You for loving me. In Jesus's name.*

ENDNOTE

1. I share more about my story of growing up in a Jewish home in my spiritual autobiography, *Awakening to Messiah*.

2

JESUS: THE WAY TO VICTORY

For you have made the Lord, my refuge,
Even the Most High, your dwelling place.
No evil will befall you,
Nor will any plague come near your tent (Psalm 91:9-10).

MY VISION OF JESUS ON THE CROSS

At the age of 20, while still deeply struggling, the Lord awoke me from a deep sleep one night. I was suddenly in a state of conscious awareness as I felt like I was being transported into another realm—a spiritual place.

In an instant, I had a supernatural vision. It was in color—I still remember it vividly to this day. In the vision, Jesus was on the cross. There were people standing in the distance, looking at Him, while He was being crucified. And all of a sudden, a ray of red light from the sky beamed down upon His head. I knew this beam of red light was coming from God, and that God was showing me that Jesus was the way to Him, because it shone from heaven and came down directly upon Jesus' head.

I knew that God had revealed Himself to me in a profound way. At that moment I knew that Jesus was the way—the only way—to the Father. The only time anyone had ever shared anything about Jesus with me before that time was when I was selling encyclopedias and a customer gave me a tract, which I immediately looked at and then threw away. I had never read the New Testament before, for the only testament for Jews is the Old Testament. I had been taught that Jesus was not for Jews. But now I knew that Jesus was the Messiah. God had revealed Himself to me, and though I didn't understand it at the time, I knew He showed me the answer to every fear and uncertainty that I was struggling with.

I started telling everyone about my vision, and someone told me to get a New Testament. After reading the New Testament, I realized that its teaching was different from my New Age books, so I threw them out. I began to devour the words of the Gospels and Paul's writings. One of the verses that really struck me during this time was John 8:32: *"And you will know the truth, and the truth will make you free."* Jesus became everything to me.

My eyes were opening to spiritual truth. There was a new freedom arising within me. I remember one day, after having been trapped in such darkness, going into a drug store to pick out a card for somebody. I picked up a card that had color on its cover. As I looked at it and saw the purple, I realized I was finally seeing colors again for the first time in over two years. My heart had been opened to see God's light.

I would go to churches and sometimes be confused by the preaching. Oftentimes they made it sound like God was not sovereign, almost as if He was wringing His hands in heaven because He had all these things He would like to do but man was in His way. I heard things like, "God is a gentleman. He will never intrude on anyone's life." I had a hard time relating to this because I knew how He had visited me supernaturally, without invitation. I also remembered what happened to Saul of Tarsus on the Road to Damascus as he was persecuting Christians, even putting some of them to death (Acts 9). But in the midst of his persecution, without invitation and without warning, Jesus showed up in glory and revealed Himself to Paul's heart.

Don't misunderstand me, God seeks our love, obedience, and cooperation, but at the end of the day, God is still God and *"He does according to His will in the host of heaven and among the inhabitants of earth"* (Dan. 4:25). The problem with some of the preaching I heard was that it made so much dependant on me and my actions, rather than on the faithfulness of God. I knew that my hope and answer rested on God's faithfulness, mercy, and love for me rather than on my ability to be perfectly obedient.

Through the Scriptures, God was showing me how much He loved me. I began to feel a strength arising within me that I had not known for years. I was now wrestling the powers of darkness, and I began to wrestle against them with the strength God gave me.

I gave myself to the Lord during this time. I devoured His Word. I memorized Bible passages. I learned how to overcome fear. The words of Isaiah accurately portray my experience: *"Do not fear, for I am with you; do not anxiously look about you, for I am your God. I will strengthen you, surely I will help you, surely I will uphold you with My righteous right hand"* (Isa. 41:10). I knew God was for me and He was with me.

UNHELPFUL HELP

My parents were not happy with this, so they enlisted the help of a deprogrammer in the hopes that he would be able to get me to turn my back on this newfound faith, which they did not understand at all. I told the deprogrammer, "I'm not programmed by anyone. I just believe that Jesus is the Messiah." My faith was rooted in a personal, supernatural revelation from the Father, so it couldn't be shaken. The people who were working to "deprogram" me soon realized I was not to be dissuaded from my faith. They continued the process by bringing me to California for two weeks, where they attempted to "rehabilitate" me.

I returned home to my parents, who were still embarrassed and angry about my stand for Jesus. Realizing the deprogramming didn't work, they brought a psychiatrist into the house to evaluate me. They must have thought that I was delusional or suffering from some kind of psychosis. The psychiatrist decided to go through the court system and have me committed to a psychiatric ward of a hospital. During that time, they tried to counsel me, including group counseling.

There was a Jewish lady in our group who was going through grief over the recent loss of her husband. She told us that he was the most wonderful man she ever knew and she was sure he was now in heaven. In a less-than-tactful manner, I blurted out, "If he didn't know Jesus, he isn't in heaven!" She seemed shocked by my response, as did the professionals there. This outburst caused them to prescribe medication to control my behavior because they said, "You are disturbing the equilibrium of the group." They also told me that if I refused to take my meds, I would be strapped down and injected with a sedative of some sort. Therefore, I decided to take the oral medication so as to avoid it being forced upon me, but I knew I did not need it.

The truth was that I was feeling so much better since Jesus had revealed Himself to me. My self-confidence was being restored, and I believed my life had a purpose and a goal again. Though my relationship with Him was fairly new, I was experiencing Him in a real way. This is not to say that I was experiencing Jesus all the time, but He was making Himself real to me in very specific ways.

After two months of hospitalization, I was interviewed by a psychiatric team, who recognized that I did not need to be there, so I was discharged and free to go. It took several months for me to recover from the hospitalization. But praise God I was soon back on my feet and continuing on with the Lord.

COMFORT FROM JESUS

Because of family issues and my faith in Jesus, I was eventually thrown out of my house. Comfort was brought to my heart as I read the words of *Yeshua Hamashiach* from the Gospel of Mark, *"I tell you the truth, no one who has left home or brothers or sisters or mother or father or children or fields for Me and the gospel will fail to receive a hundred times as much in this present age...and in the age to come, eternal life"* (Mark 10:29-30 NIV). That promise was for me.

I am also comforted as I read these words from Jesus:

> *Blessed are those who are persecuted because of righteousness, for theirs is the kingdom of heaven. Blessed are you when people insult you, persecute you and falsely say all kinds of evil against you because of Me. Rejoice and be glad, because great is your reward in heaven, for in the same way they persecuted the prophets who were before you* (Matthew 5:10-12 NIV).

My faith in Yeshua has caused and continues to cause divisions and separation between family members and me. For example, when my niece had her *bat mitzvah*, I was not even invited to participate in the ceremony with the rest of the family. Though this hurt me, it really wasn't surprising to me, because I knew from the Scriptures that the world would hate me simply because I took a stand for Jesus. Jesus said, *"They will make you outcasts from the synagogue"* (John 16:2).

Since receiving the supernatural vision of Jesus, I have faced (and withstood) significant rejection and hostility from my family and from the Jewish community in general, but my faith has remained strong. We must consider it a privilege and an honor when we are persecuted and rejected for the sake of Jesus. Though it is sometimes hard and painful to experience these breaks with family and friends, it is also a joy because God's presence becomes very near to us during these times.

The reason I'm telling you this is because many are in bondage to the fear of man. They are afraid to witness for God, to stand out, to speak up, and are controlled by their fear of being rejected by people. The Bible says that the fear of man is a snare (Prov. 29:25). The fear of man will definitely keep us from God. If I would have been controlled by a desire to be accepted and liked by my Jewish community, I would have never been able to continue on with Jesus. Many have fallen short from entering in to all that God has for them because of their fear of man. Their desire to be accepted and liked by humankind is greater than their desire to pursue God.

Jesus asked, *"How can you believe, when you receive glory from one another and you do not seek the glory that is from the one and only God?"* (John 5:44). If we are to fully lay hold of God, we must not allow our desire to be liked and accepted by others, or our fear of being persecuted or rejected, keep us from fully following Jesus. God will strengthen us in the midst of all persecution and trials.

Prayer: *Father, we pray that You will continue to reveal Your Son to us, and that we will not let any fear stand in the way of following Him. Jesus, You said that You have revealed the Father's name to Your children and that You will continue to reveal it. So we ask You to continue to reveal Yourself to us, giving us the strength and courage to follow after You without allowing fear to keep us from You.*

3

FEAR: A UNIVERSAL PROBLEM

You will not be afraid of the terror by night, or of the arrow that flies by day.... For you have made the Lord, my refuge, even the Most High, your dwelling place (Psalm 91:5,9).

CONFRONTING COMMON FEARS

In his first inaugural address, Franklin D. Roosevelt said, "The only thing we have to fear is fear itself—nameless, unreasoning, unjustified terror which paralyzes needed efforts to convert retreat into advance."[1] The common human response to fear is to retreat, hide, and cower in the shadows. But this is not God's way, beloved, for we must confront fear by advancing toward it, not retreating away from it.

In my ministry, I meet so many different people who are struggling with fear in all its varied forms. There are widows, for example, who feel so alone since they lost their husbands. Typically, these ladies have so many fears—the fear of being alone, the fear of the future, financial insecurity, health issues, and other real threats they face on a daily basis. Losing a spouse brings up many fears, both recognized and hidden.

My heart goes out to them, and I try to let each one know that they are not alone. I share Scriptures with them, showing that Jesus is with them, and He promised to never leave or forsake them. I've discovered that there are passages in the Bible that give God's answers to every fear that exists to humanity. I try to encourage God's children by speaking His words of comfort to them, such as, *"I will never desert you, nor will I ever forsake you."* This assurance of God's presence enables us to say, *"The Lord is my helper, I will not be afraid."* (Heb. 13:5-6). And in the Gospel of John Jesus said, *"I am not alone, because the Father is with Me"* (John 16:32). And the same is true for us. This is a solid answer that we must stand on if we are going to defeat fear.

Here are some other specific Scriptures that speak to common fears:

- The fear of uncertainty—*"God is our refuge and strength, a very present help in trouble. Therefore we will not fear, though the earth should change and though the mountains slip into the heart of the sea; though its waters roar and foam, though the mountains quake at its swelling pride"* (Ps. 42:1-3).

- The fear of losing everything—*"And my God will supply all your needs according to His riches in glory in Christ Jesus"* (Phil. 4:19).

- The fear of death—*"I am the resurrection and the life; he who believes in Me will live even if he dies, and every-one who lives and believes in Me will never die"* (John 11:25-26).

- The fear of the devil—*"Greater is He who is in you than he who is in the world"* (1 John 4:4). *"Behold, I have given you authority to tread on serpents and scorpions, and over all the power of the enemy, and nothing will injure you"* (Luke 10:19).

- The fear of failure—*"Abide in Me, and I in you. As the branch cannot bear fruit of itself unless it abides in the vine, so neither can you unless you abide in Me. I am the vine, you are the branches; he who abides in Me and I in him, he bears much fruit, for apart from Me you can do nothing"* (John 15:4-5).

- For every fear we may face—*"Have I not commanded you? Be strong and courageous! Do not tremble or be dismayed, for the Lord your God is with you wherever you go"* (Josh. 1:9).

Beloved, in these Scriptures and so many more throughout the Bible we find the revelation and strength we need from God's Word to overcome fear. He wants us to believe His promises, and walk in them every day of our lives. As we do this, the devil and his fears will be put to flight. We don't have to suffer from fear any longer. The Lord says, "Seize My Word and don't let anything else in." As we discipline ourselves to seize God's Word, not letting anything else in, we will become free!

SATAN: THE REAL ENEMY

In my religious training through my years at Hebrew school, I don't remember anyone ever telling me about the devil or the existence of Satan, who is the personification of evil. I knew about the concept of evil, of course, but I never knew it was personal. I was nearly sixteen years old when I saw the movie *The Exorcist*. It utterly terrified me. After seeing that movie, though, I knew there was a devil, and this knowledge scared me deeply.

I wondered, "If the devil was able to take possession of the girl in the movie (which I understood was based on a true story), how do I know he won't take possession of me in the same way?" And for months after that I would lay in my bed at night terrified. Even though I was a teenager, I would wait until I thought my parents were asleep, sneak into their room, and fall asleep on the floor by their bed. I was so afraid that the devil would take complete control of me like he did the girl in the movie.

Though I believed in the existence of God, I did not know Him in a real and personal way. However, when God revealed Himself to me and I gave my heart to Yeshua, I knew the Lord was real. I was almost instantly delivered from my fear of the devil—I knew that God had saved me and was protecting me. Beloved, the same is true for you as well. The more assured we become that we are God's, that He chose us and loves us, and because of this He is protecting us, the less afraid of the devil we will be.

OVERCOMING FEAR THROUGH LOVE

There are many steps and principles involved in finding freedom from fear that will be discussed throughout this book. But it is important to understand that freedom is available to us now, not sometime in the future. Jesus said, *"So if the Son makes you free, you will be free indeed"* (John 8:36). It is through Messiah Jesus that freedom from fear is made available to us. Again, Jesus reminds us, *"I am the way, and the truth, and the life; no one comes to the Father but through Me"* (John 14:6).

We need to take a moment to seriously think about how many of the things that we have feared have actually happened to us. How many times have we feared a sickness and never got sick? How many times have we feared a car accident only to arrive at our destination safely? How many times have we experienced nightmares only to wake up and know that it was just a dream? I ask these to point out that fears are satanic lies.

Every human being battles with fear because the enemy is constantly trying to make us afraid. He does this by casting pictures of dread into our minds regarding circumstances and relationships. He knows that when we are afraid we can no longer walk in the love of God—love and fear are at odds with each other. This is why John writes, *"There is no fear in love; but perfect love casts out fear"* (1 John 4:18).

Many think that the opposite of love is hate, but the Bible paints another picture as well. Oftentimes people hate because they're afraid. When the apostle John writes, *"There is no fear in love; but perfect love casts out fear"* (1 John 4:18), he shows us that the opposite of love is fear. We simply cannot be afraid and still walk in love at the same time. They are incompatible and contrary to one another. Therefore, if we want to walk in love and experience God's presence in a greater way, we must conquer fear, for God is love (1 John 4:18).

Fear is Satan's roadblock that prevents us from entering into our destiny as children of God. It torments us and reveals that we have not been perfected in God's love. It is not just that we have to cast it out, but rather God's love displaces it. This happens only as we enter into a deeper understanding of how loved and safe we are in God. This is why John tells us that perfect love casts out fear. In other words, the more we know how perfect God's love is for us, actively providing and protecting us, the more secure and safe we will feel. Fear will be displaced and we will be healed, rooted, and grounded in divine love.

The first words out of Adam's mouth after he partook of the fruit of the tree of the knowledge of good and evil were, *"I heard the sound of You (the Lord) in the garden, and I was afraid because I was naked; so I hid myself"* (Gen. 3:10). This biblical example helps us to see where fear comes from.

Adam had disobeyed God by eating of the fruit of the tree he was not supposed to touch. This is what we call the fall of man. After Adam fell, however, God called out to him, asking, *"Where are you, Adam?"* God, of course, knew where they were. He wasn't asking for His benefit, but so they would understand their fallen condition.

Adam responded, *"I was afraid because I was naked."* Even though Adam and Eve lived their entire existence up to this point without clothing, they suddenly felt exposed, vulnerable, and naked because of their sin. They felt unprotected and defenseless. They began to run away from God rather than toward Him.

As a result of their disobedience and sin, they were afraid. Their spiritual clothing—the godly protection they once knew—was gone. They could no longer feel the assurance of God's presence or the warmth of His love. They both felt alone and frightened. And this is what sin does to us—it separates us from God and His presence.

Ever since that event in the Garden of Eden, we have all felt alone, exposed, and naked. Though this may not be a constant feeling we are always aware of, it unconsciously plagues us.

ASSURED OF GOD'S LOVE

Ultimately, disobedience to God produces fear. The Father said to Adam and Eve, *"You shall not eat from it (the tree in the middle of the Garden) or touch it, or you will die"* (Gen. 3:3). But the serpent said to Eve, *"You surely will not die!"* (Gen. 3:4). Unfortunately, Eve believed the lie of the evil one instead of believing the words of God. This is ultimately what Adam did as well.

As a result of disobeying God's command, all humanity has lost the assurance that Adam and Eve had enjoyed in the Garden of Eden—an assurance of God's love, blessing, and presence. We all lost this beautiful paradise of peace, prosperity, health, and blessing, and we've had to earn our living by the sweat of our brow ever since.

We know that Adam and Eve did not physically die at that exact moment, but they certainly died spiritually. The day they ate of that tree the Spirit of God was removed from their lives—they were separated from Him. As their offspring, we have inherited this same condition. We now feel very vulnerable to sin, Satan, and the forces of darkness that are at work in our world. That's what happens when we feel alone; we feel extremely vulnerable to the attack of the enemy. I believe this is why people who live alone frequently die at an early age; they are unable to feel the warmth of love surrounding them.

But praise God, because of His great love for us, He has sent us His son. He does not want us to be separated from Him, or to be slaves to fear. He has provided a way of escape for us through His death and resurrection. *"It was for freedom that Christ set us free; therefore keep standing firm and do not be subject again to a yoke of slavery"* (Gal. 5:1).

Prayer: *God, I come to You today in the name of Jesus Christ the Messiah. I ask that You would empower me to overcome fear. Remove the curse that has haunted the human race ever since Adam and Eve ate of the forbidden fruit. I pray that the separation that I've experienced from You would be removed through the cross of Christ. I ask that the feelings of fear, shame, and condemnation would leave my life. And that You would help me to trust in Your love with all my heart, soul, and mind. I love You, Father, and I love You, Yeshua, and am thankful for all You have done for me. Amen.*

ENDNOTE

1. This quote was taken from FDR's first inaugural address given on March 4, 1933. It was taken from http://www.phobialist.com/fears.html, accessed on September 24, 2013.

4

DECLARING WAR ON FEAR

But Moses said to the people, "Do not fear! Stand by and
see the salvation of the Lord which He will accomplish for
you today; for the Egyptians whom you have seen today,
you will never see them again forever" (Exodus 14:13).

GOD'S COVENANTS DO NOT FAIL

The rainbow is a symbol of God's covenant that His promises will never fail. The rainbow was first given as a sign to Noah, who trusted God through the most terrifying of times—an earth-covering flood that destroyed all living creatures. What a beautiful sight it must have been to Noah each time he saw a rainbow in the sky and remembered God's faithfulness, provision, and help.

God powerfully spoke to His people through rainbows. After God destroyed everyone on the earth because of the wickedness of humanity, save Noah and his family, God gave Noah a covenant sign of a rainbow. It was to be a sign that His promises would never fail, and He would always be faithful to His Word and to His people.

And God said, "This is the sign of the covenant I am making between Me and you and every living creature with you, a covenant for all generations to come: I have set My rainbow in the clouds, and it will be the sign of the covenant between Me and the earth. Whenever I bring clouds over the earth and the rainbow appears in the clouds, I will remember My covenant between Me and you and all living creatures of every kind. Never again will the waters become a flood to destroy all life. Whenever the rainbow appears in the clouds, I will see it and remember the everlasting covenant between God and all living creatures of every kind on the earth." So God said to Noah, "This is the sign of the covenant I have established between me and all life on the earth" (Genesis 9:17 NIV).

Visions of rainbows were given to individuals throughout the Old and New Testaments. When Ezekiel saw the Lord, he described Him *"as the appearance of the rainbow in the clouds on a rainy day, so was the appearance of the surrounding radiance. Such was the appearance of the likeness of the glory of the Lord. And when I saw it, I fell on my face and heard a voice speaking"* (Ezek. 1:28). And John referred to a supernatural rainbow when describing the throne of God, *"And He who was sitting was like a jasper stone and a sardius in appearance; and there was a rainbow around the throne, like an emerald in appearance"* (Rev. 4:3).

The significance of rainbows throughout Scripture reveals to us both the glory of God's love and the covenant that we can enter into with Him through Jesus the Messiah. When Yeshua instituted the Lord's Supper,

[He] took bread, gave thanks and broke it, and gave it to His disciples, saying, "Take and eat; this is My body." Then He took the cup, gave thanks and offered it to them, saying, "Drink from it, all of you. This is my blood of the covenant,

which is poured out for many for the forgiveness of sins."
(Matthew 26:26-28 NIV).

Rainbows have been personally significant to me throughout my life. In the early eighties, I began to go through a time of repentance before the Lord. He was showing me things that I needed to turn away from in order to keep going on with Him. One of those was quitting smoking cigarettes.

One morning while I was sitting in a chair drinking a cup of tea, which had replaced the cigarettes, I had an amazing supernatural experience with the Lord. The Holy Spirit suddenly appeared above my head, twirling above me in all the colors of the rainbow. Although I couldn't see Him with my natural eyes because He was above my head, somehow I could see Him as clearly as I have ever seen anything.

He said something I did not quite understand at the time. He said, "I am a servant." I thought this meant that He was calling me to be a servant of the Lord, but I later realized that He was also saying that He is a servant. This was an amazing revelation to me. The Holy Spirit is a servant; He was sent to serve us, to teach us, and to give us comfort. Jesus said, *"I will ask the Father, and He will give you another Counselor to be with you forever—the Spirit of truth"* (John 14:16-17 NIV).

Jesus was also a servant. He said, *"I am among you as the one who serves"* (Luke 22:27). He lived His life as a servant of all humankind. He washed His disciples' feet, and He ministered to the sick, the oppressed, the downtrodden, and people from all walks of life. He spent time encouraging people through preaching and teaching. He delivered people from demons and healed them from diseases. Ultimately it was Jesus giving His life as a ransom for us, and dying a brutal death so that we might have life.

The same God who made a covenant with Noah through the rainbow appearing in the sky has entered into covenant with us today through the pouring out of Christ's blood for our redemption. And

He continues to pour Himself out for us, serving us as He strengthens, encourages, leads, and heals. We do not need to fear for we are His. We are provided for, protected and safe in Him—Jesus prayed to the Father on our behalf: *"I do not ask You to take them out of the world, but to keep them from the evil one"* (John 17:15).

WHOM SHALL I FEAR?

Just because we are protected does not mean that we will not be faced with evil and the attacks of fear. As we progress on to know the Lord in true intimacy, sometimes we experience fear even more intensely for a season. This is simply because Satan does not want us to get closer to God. He wants to lock us within the dark box of fear, paralyzing us. If yielded to, this will cause us to never fulfill our God-given potential and destiny in Christ.

After the encounter I had with the Holy Spirit in the rainbow, the Lord revealed Himself to me again in a dream, which took place right before I was married in 1982. The dream had three distinct phases.

In the first phase of the dream, I saw myself in a rectangular room that was very much like the attic of a house. It was a very dark room. There were windows on both sides. Many people, including myself, were standing against the back wall of the room. Just then the Spirit of God flowed into the room through the window that was on the right side; His form was as it had been in my earlier vision—the colors of the rainbow. He looked like living crepe paper, like the paper used to decorate a room for a party or special event, except that His form was much fuller and thicker than crepe paper. He was in all the colors of the rainbow and He was alive. It was the Spirit of Life, who manifests Himself in many ways—such as a dove (Matt. 3:16-17) and as a tongue of fire (Acts 2:1-4).

I knew this was a real encounter with the Lord and I needed to pay attention. I already had some familiarity with God communicating Himself through rainbow imagery, so I was not afraid of the experience.

All I can say is that the Lord's Spirit streamed into the room, almost like a wide, living sheet of crepe paper.

I knew that I was in the presence of the Lord's healing Spirit, so I began to walk toward Him and away from the others who were still standing against the wall. As I moved away from those huddled at the back of the room, toward the Spirit of Life, I realized that the others were staying back against the wall because fear was holding them back.

Their fear was keeping them from the rainbow of God's presence, from experiencing God in deep and powerful ways. Fear had prevented them from coming and enjoying God's manifest presence. They were in a dark room and God had manifested Himself in the form of a light—a rainbow of hope—but they were still afraid.

Even though I felt the power of fear, I kept on approaching the rainbow of God's presence with a sense of anticipation. I approached the window through which the rainbow was streaming and looked outside. The colors of the rainbow were everywhere, intensely beautiful and glorious. I opened my arms wide and asked the Spirit to come into my life. It was then that I heard the word *eternity* resounding deep within my soul.

The next phase of the dream took me to the other window in the attic-like room. When I looked out, all I could see was chaos everywhere. Nothing I saw made any sense to me. Things were moving in every direction and everything seemed random and disturbing.

That phase of my dream ended somewhat abruptly, and then I found myself walking down a street. I was peaceful and nothing was troubling my mind. But it was then that I came to an intersection where a car wreck had just taken place.

Without thinking, I walked up to the car and noticed that a man had been injured. He was lying half in the car, half out—his upper torso was lying on the street but his legs were still in the automobile. The car door was flung open and he had been badly burned. It was a terrible sight to behold.

I reached my hand toward him, and, as I did so, rainbow colors flowed from my fingertips onto his body and healed his burns. It was God's Spirit of rainbow light flowing out of my spirit, which I had received in the attic because I had not yielded to fear. Then the dream ended.

Reflecting on the dream after I woke up, I understood the others who were in the room with me were bound by fear, preventing them from receiving the rainbow Spirit of God's healing love. Instead, they cowered in the darkness, too afraid to step out by faith. They missed what God had for them because they were bound by fear. Not only did they miss out on life, but they missed out on experiencing the Author of Life.

Fear can keep us from receiving the destiny God has in store for us. It can prevent us from knowing and experiencing the love of God. Fear will prevent the rest of God from entering our souls. David declared with boldness, and Yeshua wants us to declare,

> *The Lord is my light and my salvation; whom shall I fear? The Lord is the defense of my life; whom shall I dread? When evildoers came upon me to devour my flesh, My adversaries and my enemies, they stumbled and fell. Though a host encamp against me, my heart will not fear; though war arise against me, in spite of this I shall be confident* (Psalm 27:1-3).

FAITH AND FEAR CANNOT COEXIST

Though we are to boldly declare our faith in Yeshua, the reality is that sometimes we find ourselves in fear rather than faith. Jesus said that hell was for the fearful and unbelieving (Rev. 21:8). This Scripture may cause us concern, but Yeshua's purpose in stating it is to help us understand that we must overcome fear. Notice also in this Scripture the connection between fear and unbelief, for one ultimately leads to the other.

When we are afraid, we ultimately do not believe that God is with us. This is a serious sin, for when we fear, we are not expressing faith in God, *"and whatever is not from faith is sin"* (Rom. 14:23). Faith is the channel through which God comes to us, but fear is the channel through which Satan gains entrance into our lives. If we replace the bridge of fear leading to satanic activity with the bridge of faith leading to God, we will experience God's peace and love. You see, even as we access God by faith, we access darkness by fear. Faith in God leads to experiencing the reality of His presence and love. Fear, on the other hand, opens us up to be tormented by Satan and the realm of darkness.

The writer of Hebrews said that *without faith it is impossible to please Him, for he who comes to God must believe that He is and that He is a rewarder of those who seek Him*" (Heb. 11:6). When we're afraid, we don't believe God is at work in our lives and present with us. This creates a general anxiety in our hearts that prevents us from moving on with God and from doing what He has asked us to do. But Paul speaks powerfully into our lives when he says, *"Be anxious for nothing, but in everything by prayer and supplication with thanksgiving let your requests be made known to God"* (Phil. 4:6).

There should be no fear in our lives when we are living in a close, personal relationship with God. More than a hundred times throughout the Scriptures God commands us to not be afraid. It is important to note that it is a command, not an option for us to choose whether or not we're going to obey. God reminds us, *"Be strong and courageous! Do not tremble or be dismayed, for the Lord your God is with you wherever you go"* (Josh. 1:9).

There is no room for fear in our lives when we are obeying this direct command from our heavenly Father. Fear is a spiritual sin that goes deeper than the sins of the flesh. It is not a sin because of what we're afraid of; it is a sin because we've replaced faith in God with faith in other things, believing they have more influence and power in our lives than God does. It causes us to bow down to Satan. When we fear this or that, live in habitual anxiety or a state of dread, we are living in sin by magnifying Satan in our hearts rather than God and His goodness. In fearing we are agreeing that Satan is more powerful than God.

When we fear we are revealing that we don't really trust God and, in fact, are expressing more faith in Satan and evil. This, beloved, is not God's will for us.

Trust and fear are opposed to each other. One cannot live in a state of fear and trust God. It's impossible to do so. *Trust in the Lord with all your heart and do not lean on your own understanding. In all your ways acknowledge Him, and He will make your paths straight"* (Prov. 3:5-6).

FEAR IS BEHIND EVERY NEGATIVE EMOTION

We can't experience God's love, peace, and rest in our lives and continue to walk in fear. Fear will not produce love, peace, and rest, but rather anxiety, hate, and jealously. The truth is that fear underlies most negative emotions we experience in our lives. For example, often when an employer gets angry with an employee, at the root it is because he or she is afraid of losing money, prestige, or position within the company. Likewise, a parent could feel that other parents may look down on them because they feel that their child is not measuring up in some way. This fear may cause a parent to express anger toward their child. In these cases, as in so many others, fear is the driving factor behind the behavior.

To walk in fear and thus anger is to walk away from God, who is love. Which would we rather experience on a daily basis—the coldness and anger that fear produces or the peaceful experience of God's presence and love? We don't have to live in fear any longer, beloved; through Christ Jesus we can be free.

DECLARE WAR ON FEAR

There are two Hebrew words for fear used throughout the Bible. The first is *yahreh*, which means "dread"—to dread or to be frightened of—and the second is *aratz*, which is the term that is used in Joshua 1:9, meaning "to tremble at."

The Lord commanded Joshua not to tremble at the hostile armies surrounding him: *"Do not tremble, Joshua, or be dismayed, for the Lord your God is with you."* This same message is for every one of us today, no matter what forces might be threatening us at this time. We may even see storm clouds gathering on the horizon, but we must resist being shaken because God is with us and for us.

Like Joshua, we must resist all temptations to fear by finding courage and refuge in the Lord. We must wake up and fight fear with the weapons the Lord has given us—His Word, the name and blood of Jesus, and the power of the Holy Spirit. We must also remember that He is fighting the battle with us and for us.

When Moses was about to cross the Red Sea with the Egyptians hot on Israel's tail, Moses said to Israel, *"Do not fear! Stand by and see the salvation of the Lord which He will accomplish for you today; for the Egyptians whom you have seen today, you will never see them again forever"* (Exod. 14:13). And to Jehoshaphat, God said, *"'You need not fight in this battle; station yourselves, stand and see the salvation of the Lord on your behalf, O Judah and Jerusalem.' Do not fear or be dismayed; tomorrow go out to face them, for the Lord is with you"* (2 Chron. 20:17).

It is time that we become proactive wielding the Word of God in our fight against fear. We must shake off passivity. It is time to fight, not to yield; to be on the offensive, not the defensive. We must put on the whole armor of God, which will shield us from fear, standing our ground in Messiah (Eph. 6). Having done our part, we can stand still, trusting in God's love and grace knowing that He is going before us and working on our behalf.

Joshua obeyed God even though hostile forces were surrounding him. He chose to be strong and take courage; not to be fearful, dismayed, terrified, or anxious. He believed God, beloved, and you and I can too. As a result, Joshua was able to lead his people, the children of Israel, into their God-given inheritance.

If we want to receive and enter our destiny as God's children, we must learn to resist all fear in its varied forms. Indeed, we must declare war on it, not tolerating it even for a second. God wants us to experience and possess the fullness of the Holy Spirit.

Though the enemy will attack us, we must not give in, for *"greater is He who is in you than he who is in the world"* (1 John 4:4). We must resist him: *"Submit yourselves, then, to God. Resist the devil and he will flee from you"* (James 4:8 NIV). We are not to flee from the devil in fear, but to stand, go on the offense, and cause him to flee from us through faith! As we do, the shalom and love of God fills us.

LET US NOT COWER IN FEAR

What kept the Israelites wandering in the wilderness forty years? Was it not fear itself? When the spies went into the land of Canaan and came back to report what was in it, they told the children of Israel that the land was filled with good things. But they quickly added that it was also filled with giants (Num. 13). As a result of focusing on the giants rather than magnifying God, the people cowered in fear. This caused the Lord to be angry with them which resulted in forty years of wandering.

In much the same way, people today are cowering in the face of confusion, chaos, and the dangers that surround them. Financial crises, terrorist attacks, natural disasters, violence, accidents, poisonous substances, pestilences, diseases, social fears, contaminated foods, and other potential disasters seem to be everywhere we look. Some people are afraid to even leave their homes.

Regardless of where you are in this spectrum, God's Word to you is the same: "Do not be afraid, for I am with you wherever you go." Knowing this, that God loves us, that He is all-powerful, and perfectly, actively involved in the details of our lives, is all we really need to know, beloved, in order to be free from fear. He is the God who is always with us. Wherever you go, He is there.

We need to come to the place where we actively believe that God is bigger than our problem, no matter what that problem might be. Though Satan is crouching at the door and desiring to fill us with fear, we must resist him and cling to Messiah Jesus.

By quoting from the Book of Deuteronomy, Jesus defeated the assault of the enemy in the wilderness (Luke 4:1-13). In the same way, we can defeat darkness and fear today by believing in and trusting in God's Word for ourselves. As God was with Israel, so He is with us, His people today. *"Hear, O Israel, you are approaching the battle against your enemies today. Do not be fainthearted. Do not be afraid, or panic, or tremble before them, for the Lord your God is the one who goes with you, to fight for you against your enemies, to save you"* (Deut. 20:3-4). Living in fear grieves the heart of God. Why does living in fear grieve the heart of God? When we fear, we reveal that we believe Satan rather than Him. When the devil comes to us and puts all kinds of lying thoughts and images into our mind, we need to reject those foul imaginations and remember God's Word and His trustworthiness. To do otherwise is to magnify Satan instead of magnifying God.

Imagine Satan going before God with his lying accusations about you. "See, he really doesn't believe in You. He's bowing down to me. His allegiance is to me because he is trapped in fear." But thank God that we have an advocate with the Father, who is Jesus Christ the righteous. He pleads our case before the Father, but He wants us to cooperate with Him and to take a stand against lies, fear, and Satan.

FEAR DOESN'T ADD TO LIFE

Jesus said that living in fear and worry doesn't add one cubit to our life (Matt. 6:27). In other words, when we are afraid of something, it does us no good. All it does is rob us of experiencing God's presence today. Worse yet, we can actually attract to ourselves the things we fear.

FEAR IS A FORM OF REBELLION

There is a sense in which we could say that fear is a form of rebellion. In Numbers 14 we read these words of warning from Joshua:

> *The land which we passed through to spy out is an exceedingly good land. If the Lord is pleased with us, then He will bring us into this land and give it to us—a land which flows with milk and honey.* **Only do not rebel against the Lord; and do not fear the people of the land,** *for they will be our prey. Their protection has been removed from them, and the Lord is with us; do not fear them* (Numbers 14:7-9).

Why is fear is a form of rebellion? It's because it causes us to choose not to believe God and His Word. Instead, we choose to believe the lies of Satan. We need to stop trusting what we see with our natural eyes, for the world and all that is in it is passing away. We need to stop being deceived by what we hear as well. Instead, we need to seize God and His Word.

The yoke of fear will be broken off of our lives as we turn to God. Divine power, revelation, divine electricity, and the energy of the Holy Spirit are ours through Christ. Jesus said, *"The thief comes only to steal and kill and destroy; I came that they may have life, and have it abundantly"* (John 10:10). Abundant life, which is a life free from fear, can be yours today.

Prayer: *Dear Father in heaven, forgive me for my fears and help me to overcome them through the power of Your Word, Your Spirit, and by drawing close to You. I will spend time in Your presence each day, and I will sit at Your footstool and learn of You. I thank You, Yeshua, that You are always waiting for me. You are always with me, and You are the same yesterday, today, and forever.*

5

KNOWING GOD IS WITH US

He who dwells in the shelter of the Most High will
abide in the shadow of the Almighty (Psalm 91:1).

GOD LIKES US

Many of us know God loves us, but do we know that He also likes us? He really does. He not only loves us, but He actually likes us and wants to be with us. In Exodus 25, the Lord told Moses to build a tabernacle so that He could dwell with the children of Israel. God actually wanted to be with them, to have fellowship with them. Jesus said in Revelation 3:20, *"Behold I stand at the door and knock; if anyone hears My voice and opens the door, I will come in to him and will dine with him, and he with Me."* God loves us, likes us, and enjoys having fellowship with us. My prayer for us is that we will understand these realities.

Paul prayed that the Holy Spirit would direct our hearts into the love of God:

May the Lord direct your hearts into the love of God and
into the steadfastness of Christ (2 Thessalonians 3:5).

So that Christ may dwell in your hearts through faith; and that you, being rooted and grounded in love, may be able to comprehend with all the saints what is the breadth and length and height and depth, and to know the love of Christ which surpasses knowledge, that you may be filled up to all the fullness of God (Ephesians 3:17-19).

Knowing that God loves us and likes us is foundational in eradicating fear from our life. And we can only come to know His great love for us through the power of the Holy Spirit at work within us. The encounters I've mentioned in previous chapters have created a passion within me to seek the reality of God's presence in my life. I don't want to have to wait until I get to heaven to experience His presence; I want it in the here and now.

Having an assurance that He is always with us will block fear from our life. David wrote, *"You will make known to me the path of life; in Your presence is fullness of joy; in Your right hand there are pleasures forever"* (Ps. 16:11). We can walk in God's presence and experience His joy and pleasures on a day-to-day basis. God has made Himself available to us now, while on earth. The abundant life we can experience in Him isn't just for heaven; it is also for now.

We must never forget that the Holy Spirit dwells within us. This is a real scientific fact and spiritual reality. Paul actually says that, *"But if the Spirit of Him who raised Jesus from the dead dwells in you, He who raised Christ Jesus from the dead will also give life to your mortal bodies through His Spirit who dwells in you"* (Rom. 8:11). What this means is that God's Spirit is literally dwelling inside us, releasing health and divine life into our mind and mortal bodies.

In Acts 2, when the Spirit was first given, we read that the disciples who received Him spoke in languages that they had no knowledge of. How is this possible? It is because a special and holy entity, the Spirit of the living God, actually took up habitation within them, giving them a supernatural life that they previously did not possess. This supernatural life that was now residing within them gave them supernatural abilities. This same Spirit is now dwelling in you to empower you to know God's presence and to overcome fear.

INCREASING FELLOWSHIP

As I began to grow in the Lord, I tried many things to draw closer to Him. I would pray three hours a day, read and memorize my Bible, and give more than a tithe to the Lord. I attended church faithfully and was constantly witnessing to people.

Once I heard a teaching that said the key to intimacy with God was found in praying the Lord's Prayer (Matt. 6:9-13), so I started praying this model prayer of Jesus at least fifteen minutes a day. I increased it to thirty minutes a day; then I went on to praying it for an hour each day. But nothing different was taking place as a result of praying the Lord's Prayer. So I decided to start praying it two hours a day, and then finally three hours a day! Still it seemed like nothing was changing. I was doing all I knew to do. However, God's presence still seemed far away. Although I had several supernatural experiences with the Lord, I was not experiencing intimacy with Him on a daily basis.

Then I thought that perhaps I was talking to God too much. So I would pray for an hour and a half and then listen for an hour and a half. Still nothing happened. So I decided to try sitting and listening for three hours. I fell asleep.

I desperately wanted intimacy with God, but I was beginning to get burned out in my pursuit. Sometime later I sensed God speaking to my spirit, "You're looking for Me on the outside; but I'm *inside* you. I want you to learn to sit before Me, be still, and let go of everything in your life. I only want you to look to Me for one thing—the revelation that My Spirit is dwelling within you."

That word from the Lord spoke volumes to me. It changed my entire perspective and outlook on life. Everything in my life began to change, and a new power—the power of the Holy Spirit—infused my being. The revelation of God's Spirit within me opened the door to greater intimacy with Him, enabling me to walk in greater power and authority. I pray that my sharing this will strengthen this reality that Christ dwells in you.

THE GIFT OF THE RUACH HAKODESH

The *Ruach HaKodesh* (the Holy Spirit) has taken up residence in our lives as believers. Through the Holy Spirit Jesus lives within us. Paul reminds us of this when he writes, *"The mystery which has been hidden from the past ages and generations, but has now been manifested to His saints...which is Christ* [Messiah] *in you, the hope of glory"* (Col. 1:26-27). And Jesus said God's rule and reign isn't somewhere out there, but rather *"the kingdom of God is within you"* (Luke 17:21 NIV). As new believers we believe in a Jesus residing in heaven, but spiritual maturity takes place when we learn and come to experience that He is also within us.

Approximately one year after I received the vision of Messiah Jesus on the cross, I had another major spiritual encounter with the Lord. Whether it was a vision, dream, or something else I cannot say. All I know is that God opened up the spirit realm to me and allowed me to see into the heavenlies late one night.

God allowed me to see two spirits. The first was shaped like an egg—sealed and self-contained. This egg-like spirit, which I believed to be the Holy Spirit, appeared to be two and a half to three feet long and a foot and a half high and wide. Every part of Him was in constant motion, and bubbled up with pure, white, eternal life. His perfectly coordinated motion reminded me of a friend of mine from high school who was a fantastic dancer and moved with beautiful rhythm and symmetry.

This Spirit of Everlasting Life was entirely surrounded by darkness, however. This was a darker darkness than I'd ever seen before, much more intense than simply being the absence of light. The spirit of darkness was also alive and in motion. It moved in an entirely different way than the Spirit of Life moved. They both were alive, but they were very different life forms and were in opposition to each other. The spirit of darkness was moving in random spurts, and it was not flowing beautifully like God's Spirit was.

I believe that the spirit of white life that I saw is the Holy Spirit that is given to and indwells each believer. This is why it is so important that we cultivate a sense of God's presence within us instead of always looking for Him somewhere outside ourselves. God was showing me that I would find the Spirit of Life within me, not on the outside where darkness dwells; and that the Spirit of Life would give me energy, power, victory, and peace. Through this experience I realized that we all need to be led by God's indwelling Spirit rather than by the darkness of the world around us.

Once we allow God's Spirit to be our life force, we will enter into a rest in Him, and a peace that surpasses all understanding. We will not have to struggle in the flesh any longer. We will learn to trust God, knowing that He is with us, going before us, working on our behalf, and helping us to be victorious. Knowing that you don't have to control everything, that it doesn't all depend on you, and that you can trust God, releases many burdens and produces rest.

The Holy Spirit is the key to knowing that God is always with us. This is why Yeshua said, *"But I tell you the truth: It is for your good that I am going away. Unless I go away, the Counselor* (the Holy Spirit) *will not come to you; but if I go, I will send Him to you"* (John 16:7 NIV). Jesus also said to His disciples concerning the Holy Spirit, "He lives with you and will be in you" (John 14:17 NIV). Knowing the reality of Jesus living within us gives us the security we need to break the strongholds of fear. As we get deeper and deeper into the time that the Bible calls "the last days," it will be more crucial than ever to lay hold of the reality that Jesus lives within us by His Spirit.

TOOLS TO DEAL WITH FEAR

We are living in the end times, beloved, which means the presence of fear is increasing because calamities are becoming more frequent. Jesus spoke of this time, saying that people will be *"fainting from fear and the expectation of the things which are coming upon the world; for the powers of the heavens will be shaken"* (Luke 21:26). We see this prophecy being fulfilled in our present age, which means the end of time is coming soon. As the world becomes more unstable, people will become less secure and their hearts will be engulfed with fear. The world is becoming more chaotic, violent, fearful, and lawless.

Jesus said that these things would occur. He called it *"the beginning of sorrows"* (Matt. 24:8 KJV). These "sorrows" will continue to increase as Satan devises new ways to attack humanity. In light of this, it's important for us not to keep our fears to ourselves. We must talk about our fears instead of keeping them buried within. By so doing we can externalize our fears instead of owning them and internalizing them. Opening up about our fears is sometimes the first step in the deliverance process.

The enemy tries to cause us to be afraid to talk about what we are afraid of. We need to learn to bring our fears into the light and stop hiding them. We are not to be afraid of fear, and we are not to be afraid of opening up to those God is calling us to confide in. In fact, the Lord will actually cleanse us from our fears as we share them with others. Scripture tells us, *"If we confess our sins* [including the sin of fear], *He is faithful and righteous to forgive us our sins and to cleanse us from all unrighteousness"* (1 John 1:9).

BE PREPARED FOR THE ENEMY'S ATTACK

Beloved, even as I'm sharing with you specific action steps that you can take to know God better, I want you to be aware that as you draw closer to God the enemy will attack.

I remember a time about thirty years ago when I was spending a great deal of time seeking the Lord. It was an intense pursuit and it took all of my time. I was encouraged and motivated by a verse in Hebrews that God *"is a rewarder of those who seek Him"* (Heb. 11:6). I felt that the more I sought God, the more He would reward me.

On one particular day after I had spent the whole day seeking the Lord, I was excited about what my reward might be. I greatly looked forward to what He was going to do. However, in my sleep that night, I experienced an incredibly violent attack, in which the forces of evil assaulted me relentlessly, viciously, and angrily. The enemy's rage was palpable, and I knew he hated me and wanted to kill me. I felt like I was a dodgeball being violently bounced back and forth against the hard walls of my room.

When I woke up, I knew I had been spiritually attacked by the forces of darkness. The experience was so horrendous that the thought came to mind, "Maybe you shouldn't be seeking God so much if this is going to happen to you." The devil was trying to make me afraid to seek God for fear of the repercussions that would take place if I did. Beloved, always resist messages such as these from the enemy.

When we begin to seek God in earnest, the enemy may attack using strong fear tactics, but we cannot give in. We are to keep on keeping on, never giving up on our pursuit of God.

In 2006, I was going through a crisis in my life. The Lord began working in my life in a special way. He was separating me unto Himself. During this time Yeshua gave me a supernatural grace to listen to worship music for hours on end each day, soaking up His presence.

At this same time I was ministering once a week for eight weeks at a church in Michigan. It was a large congregation and the services were going well. Each evening, though, prior to ministering, a feeling of great dread would come over me. I could not even identify what the fear was; I just knew it was present. I tried to shake it off, but it kept coming back every night before I would minister.

I now understand that as I was moving deeper into the Lord, the enemy was trying to throw up a roadblock in front of me, and that roadblock came to me in the form of fear. The devil sometimes tries to intrude in our lives when we are seeking God with abandon. Yes, God is our shield, but He wants us to know how ferocious the enemy is at times.

To the children of Israel God had said, "I've given you this land." But it was their responsibility to drive out the enemies who lived there, which were the Hittites, the Jebusites, and the Canaanites. We must do the same with our enemy today. The Lord could have gotten rid of these enemies for them, but He wanted the Israelites to be involved in the process.

STEADFASTNESS

Jesus has set us free, but we must enter into and maintain our freedom by standing on the promises of God's Word and fighting fear with tenacity. Jesus said seven times in the Book of Revelation, *"he who overcomes"* will inherit His promises. He has set us free, but our responsibility (our response to His ability) is to overcome by standing firm in the faith. *"For whatever is born of God overcomes the world; and this is the victory that has overcome the world—our faith"* (1 John 5:4).

God makes us complete as we engage in the battle against the enemy. This is not optional in our growth as a Christian. It is a real fight to be engaged in on a continual basis. It won't go away until we face it and defeat it by the power and authority of Jesus dwelling within us and God's Word. We must fight with steadfastness.

AN UNSAFE WORLD

The Bible repeatedly tells us not to be afraid, and yet when we look around us, we see real dangers and can experience real fears. We see car accidents taking place, and so we fear for our children and grandchildren as they are driving. We see numerous illnesses affecting the lives of people we know, so we therefore become afraid of sicknesses and diseases.

We see people dying before their time, and we hear of economic woes affecting millions.

We hear of terrorist acts taking place around the world, and governments warning us about cyber attacks and sabotaging electrical grids. It seems that dangers lurk around every corner, and the world seems to be spiraling out of control. Riots are taking place in many nations, and people are killing each other. Suicides are on the rise. Financial instability has increased. It is a time of great upheaval, and the world is a very unsafe place.

We may ask ourselves in the midst of all of this, "Why shouldn't I be afraid? These things could happen to me." Beloved, without the Lord solidifying us on the inside, we will be afraid in this unsafe world. Negative news reports, horror films, some political speeches, and the media all contribute to this fear. These negative stimuli can take our focus off of God who resides with us.

"Christ in you, the hope of glory" (Col. 1:27) means our focus should be upon Him living within us and empowering us rather than focusing on the outside world and the forces of darkness surrounding us. I recommend abstaining from all negative media and *"fixing our eyes on Jesus, the author and perfecter of* [our] *faith"* (Heb. 12:2).

Addictions to texting, Facebook, e-mail, television, or the newspaper draw us outside of Jesus and ourselves and focus us on the wrong things. The Scripture says, *"Finally, brethren, whatever is true, whatever is honorable, whatever is right, whatever is pure, whatever is lovely, whatever is of good repute, if there is any excellence and if anything worthy of praise, dwell on these things"* (Phil. 4:8).

Beloved, as we examine ourselves, are we dwelling on good things, or are we worrying? We must be more in tune with God's indwelling Spirit than the world around us. We must keep eternity's values in view and not worry about the things of tomorrow. Jesus tells us:

For this reason I say to you, do not be worried about your life, as to what you will eat or what you will drink; nor for your body, as to what you will put on. Is not life more than food, and the body more than clothing? Look at the birds of the air, that they do not sow, nor reap nor gather into barns, and yet your heavenly Father feeds them. Are you not worth much more than they? And who of you by being worried can add a single hour to his life? (Matthew 6:25-27)

God is always with us; He will not fail us. We must trust Him with our finances, our health, our family, our job, our career, and our future. He will never let us down, for He is always with us and will never leave us.

Prayer: *Lord, I thank You that You love me and like me! I pray that You would keep me safe, secure, and steadfast in You. I ask for You to help me remain in You, Jesus, and in Your Word. Help me to overcome my fears. I believe that through Your power and by Your grace I can overcome the world. I love You, Jesus.*

6

DWELLING UNDER THE SHADOW OF THE MOST HIGH

He who dwells in the shelter of the Most High
Will abide in the shadow of the Almighty. I will
say to the Lord, "My refuge and my fortress, My
God, in whom I trust!" (Psalm 91:1-2)

PSALM 91

We overcome fear by exercising faith in the Word of God. I have struggled with fear throughout my life, and I still do. But the struggles are very different than they used to be, and I'm operating on a different level of victory. Many of the fears that I used to have—the fear of death, for example—are gone. But Satan will continually project other scenarios onto the screen of my mind seeking to ensnare me. Yet God is continually showing me how to overcome and conquer fear.

Psalm 91 is a passage that I've committed to memory and it has strengthened me in my ability to keep the door of my heart closed to fear. In Psalm 91 we read of God's protection from everything that could harm us.

Some time ago I was sitting in my study getting ready for a prayer meeting, I prayed, "Lord, if I can really believe that you will do for me what Psalm 91 says you do, then I'm going to randomly open my Bible. If when I open it, it opens to Psalm 91, then I'll take that to mean that I can believe You will do for me what Psalm 91 says You do."

Well, beloved, do you know what happened? I went into the sanctuary, randomly opened my Bible up, and there was Psalm 91. I want to encourage you to believe God for what He says He does for His children in this psalm.

A VERSE-BY-VERSE LOOK

When fighting fear, this Psalm can be a real source of victory as we believe in God's protection over us. So let's take a closer look at it, verse by verse.

He who dwells in the shelter of the Most High will abide in the shadow of the Almighty. (Psalm 91:1)

If we dwell in the shelter of the Most High, clinging to the Lord, and totally depending on Him, and if we are walking humbly, we will be able to abide in the shelter of the Almighty. His shelter is our safe place and our place of refuge in an unsafe world. If we fail to do this on a daily basis, we will be vulnerable to all the enemy's devices and attacks.

To walk in protection, then, we must dwell in the shelter of the Most High and abide in the shadow of the Almighty. We do this through prayer, reading His Word, and clinging to Him throughout our day. If we do otherwise, we will become a bull's-eye for the enemy's fiery darts. We must be a people who set our mind and spirit to dwell in God continually, for this is our protection and our covering.

I will say to the Lord, "My refuge and my fortress, my God, in whom I trust!" (Psalm 91:2).

We will not have fear in our lives if we truly trust the Lord in everything (Prov. 3:5-6). God has placed a hedge of protection around us. He has erected a fortress to keep us safe from all attacks as long as our heart is focused upon Him. I'm not saying that we don't get attacked, but that we are secure as we abide in Him. When we are within that fortress, we are safe in God's presence.

Notice that this is not a passive faith; it is an active, aggressive, and proactive belief in our God. Our response to His command to be "strong and courageous" cannot be passive. We must make a declaration right now to be strong and courageous, saying, "I will trust in the Lord. I will not fear. He is my fortress and my refuge." We can pray to Him, "I'm going to trust You, Lord. I make up my mind, Father, to stop betraying You through a lack of trust. I take my stand upon Your Word, and I choose to stand with You. Father, I believe; help me in my unbelief. And strengthen my faith in You and in Your Word. In the name of Yeshua, amen."

For it is He who delivers you from the snare of the trapper and from the deadly pestilence (Psalm 91:3).

Satan is a trapper, seeking to catch us in his devices, but Father is watching over us, protecting us, and delivering us. This is absolute. There is no weapon that Satan forms against us that Father is not aware of and not able to handle. He is actively involved in delivering and protecting us every day. We are His little children, and He is constantly watching over us. Jesus prayed, *"Keep* [My disciples] *from the evil one"* (John 17:15). And He taught us to pray, *"And do not lead us into temptation, but deliver us from evil"* (Matt. 6:13).

He will cover you with His pinions, and under His wings you may seek refuge; His faithfulness is a shield and bulwark (Psalm 91:4).

Our faithful Father will cover us with His wings like a mother hen covers her chicks. When Jesus was on a boat with His disciples, a fierce storm blew up, and the men were fearful. Jesus was not worried, however, and He calmed the winds and waves with His words.

Jesus Himself was in the stern, asleep on the cushion; and they woke Him and said to Him, "Teacher, do You not care that we are perishing?" And He got up and rebuked the wind and said to the sea, "Hush, be still." And the wind died down and it became perfectly calm. And He said to them, "Why are you afraid? How is it that you have no faith?" They became very much afraid and said to one another, "Who then is this, that even the wind and the sea obey Him?" (Mark 4:38-41)

Jesus is with us in everything that we go through. And His faithfulness to us is what gives us security and ensures our safety. At times, like the disciples on the boat, we experience the wind and the waves, but Yeshua is always with us, and will see us safely through every storm that life throws at us. We must come to the place that we are not afraid of facing difficulty because we know that Yeshua will bring us safely through it.

One of the keys to overcoming fear is knowing that Yeshua is faithful in the midst of the winds and the waves. He will never let us down, so we don't have to be afraid of trouble. Great victories and peace come to us when we come to the place where we no longer panic when something goes wrong. Jesus will always bring us victoriously through, even as He did the disciples on the boat. His faithfulness is a shield and a bulwark that nothing from the enemy can ever penetrate. When fear tries to attack us, we are safe under His wings.

You will not be afraid of the terror by night, or of the arrow that flies by day. Of the pestilence that stalks in darkness, or of the destruction that lays waste at noon (Psalm 91:5-6).

Here the Lord is speaking directly to our fears. He is saying that He is with us both night and day. He never slumbers nor sleeps, beloved. He is always with us, constantly aware of everything that we are going through. He knows when we're fearful or when we're anxious. And He is the One who delivers us. We don't need to keep our nightlight on, or the television on in our room at night. We do not need to worry about anything at all. Why? Because God is with us, beloved, and He will never let us down. We don't have to fear.

Not too long ago I was outside and something smelled good, so I took in the pleasant smell, breathing deeply, inhaling the fragrance. I later realized the farmer across the street was spraying his fields with something. I wondered what he was doing. A few days later I drove by his field and saw that everything in it was completely dead. The pleasant smell I was enjoying turned out to be weed killer. I became fearful knowing that I had breathed that poison in.

It was faith in the Word of God that got me over that fear. We don't have be afraid of any deadly pestilence, for Jesus said, *"These signs will accompany those who have believed: in My name they will cast out demons, they will speak with new tongues; they will pick up serpents, and if they drink any deadly poison, it will not hurt them; they will lay hands on the sick, and they will recover"* (Mark 16:17-18). And a firm trust in the Word of God is what will get us through all our fears.

> *A thousand may fall at your side and ten thousand at your right hand, but it shall not approach you* (Psalm 91:7).

One of the greatest obstacles that I've had on my faith journey is perceiving God based on my perception of other people's lives and situations as opposed to simply taking a hold of His Word. In other words, as I've said before, I would see many around me experiencing destruction and as a result I would feel vulnerable, assuming that if it happened to them, it could happen to me. But when I went to my Bible and it opened to Psalm 91, I knew that Father was telling me I could trust Him regardless of the fact that others were falling. This is a very personal promise, and trusting in the truth of it is absolutely necessary to find freedom and victory over fear.

You will look on with your eyes and see the recompense of the wicked (Psalm 91:8).

A recompense is a payment or a compensation that is given to someone for what they have done. We will see the wicked receive what they deserve. We do not have to fear that evil people will win; God will vindicate us, for He always does. Eternity will put everything in order. In some situations the "last shall be first and the first last" (Matt. 20:16).

*For you have made the Lord, my refuge, even the Most High,
your dwelling place* (Psalm 91:9).

Here we see God reinforcing another important truth:. We are to abide in the dwelling place of God. Jesus echoed this part of the psalm when He said,

*Abide in Me, and I in you. As the branch cannot bear fruit of
itself unless it abides in the vine, so neither can you unless you
abide in Me. I am the vine, you are the branches; he who abides
in Me and I in him, he bears much fruit, for apart from me
you can do nothing. If you abide in Me, and My words abide
in you, ask whatever you wish, and it will done for you* (John
15:4-5,7).

There is a place where we can abide so deeply in God that no harm can come near us.

No evil will befall you, nor will any plague come near your tent
(Psalm 91:10).

I want you to get this, beloved, and to remember it forever—no evil will befall you. You will face evil, but you will always overcome. Are you afraid for your family (those who dwell within your tent)? Then you must believe that no evil and no plague will come near you or your tent. This is God's promise to us, so let's believe God for our families. He wants to bless us and those we love, and He will do so according to the promise of

His Word. We can count on Him to always be faithful to everything He has ever said to us.

> *For He will give His angels charge concerning you, to guard you in all your ways. They will bear you up in their hands, that you do not strike your foot against a stone.* (Psalm 91:11-12)

Angelic protection is a wonderful thing that is part of our inheritance in Christ. Angels are ministering spirits that come to us when we are in need. We have no idea how many times they have helped us, but we can be assured that they have. The writer of Hebrews said that we should continue to show hospitality to strangers, *"for by this some have entertained angels without knowing it"* (Heb. 13:2).

Angels are warriors and they are helping us in every spiritual battle we face, whether we see them or not. They are guarding us even when we don't know they are there. Angels are here to help us and to keep us from falling. They are with us as we are driving down the road, and unbeknownst to us they may have protected us many times from accidents and other calamities. Thank God for His angels, who are assigned to protect us and guard us.

Years ago at college, I met a couple whose mission was to disciple new believers. I was a new believer, and this couple sought to bring me into their home, employ me in their carpet-cleaning business, and disciple me. They asked to meet my parents. So we drove from Columbus, Ohio, where I was attending college at the time, to Cleveland, Ohio, where my parents lived.

Keep in mind that I'm a Jewish boy who grew up in an affluent area. We drove up in the dilapidated vehicle they owned. Upon entering my house, we sat down at the kitchen table with my parents, who are already extremely upset with my decision for Jesus. And now this couple told them that they wanted to bring me into their home, disciple me, and bring me into their carpet-cleaning business. It was at this point that I was suddenly able to hear in the spirit world and I heard the angels speak. I don't know what the angels said, but I just heard beautiful singing from heaven. They were emotionally protecting me from the oppressive environment I found myself in.

> *You will tread upon the lion and cobra, the young lion and the serpent you will trample down* (Psalm 91:13).

Take a moment to ponder the truth of this powerful verse. God will give us the power to tread upon evil and even Satan himself. We will be able to trample him under our feet. Paul encouraged the Romans and said, *"The God of peace will soon crush Satan under your feet"* (Rom. 16:20). We are mighty in God and are not to fear evil.

Before knowing Jesus, I was terrified of the devil (after seeing *The Exorcist*), afraid to be in the home alone, afraid at night, but now I'm free through Messiah Jesus! It is important to remember, *"greater is He who is in you than he who is in the world"* (1 John 4:4).

> *Because he has loved Me, therefore I will deliver him; I will set him securely on high because he has known My name. He will call upon Me, and I will answer him; I will be with him in trouble; I will rescue him and honor him* (Psalm 91:14-15).

God will deliver us from all fear because we love Him, and He will set us on high because we know the power of His name. But let us not forget, we love Him because He first loved us. We know His name only because He has revealed Himself to us. It is all grace! Paul said that we were set in heavenly places when we were born again (Eph. 2:4-6); therefore, we need to ask God to help us view the world from His perspective where there is no fear.

The first part of this verse is a prayer promise. God hears us when we pray and, more importantly, He answers our prayers. He is with us even when we are in trouble, and He promises to rescue us and even to honor us.

Many of you have gone through or may be going through situations in your job where you feel you have been treated unfairly. I want to encourage you to trust God in the midst of your situation. He will rescue you and honor you as you cling to Him.

> *With a long life I will satisfy him and let him see My salvation.*
> (Psalm 91:16)

This psalm concludes with the promise that we will see God's glory and victory manifest in our lives. Satan's fears are a lie, but Jesus came to give life and to give it more abundantly.

CAN BAD THINGS STILL HAPPEN?

Do you ever find yourself wondering why terrible things still happen to some believers in spite of what Psalm 91 says? What do we do when bad things happen to God's people? Are we tempted to doubt and not believe His Word? To discount His promises?

I know some believers, for example, who seem to be constantly living in failure. Everything in their lives seems broken; nothing seems to work out for them. The promises of God are seemingly not being fulfilled in their lives; everything seems to be in a shambles. How do we deal with a situation like this?

For a long time I did not know how to face this type of scenario. I tried to ignore it, but I came to the point where I had to get answers to this perplexing question. I had an experience one cold and icy night when I was ministering with a team in a church. The service went well, but after it was over, a member of the team came running up to me and said, "My wife fell in the parking lot. Please come and pray for her. She's in the car, groaning."

I said, "Lord, what is going on here? This lady just finished ministering for You. I know You cause all things to work together for good, but couldn't You have kept her from falling? Where were the angels that You promised would bear her up? Please give me an answer. Why does it seem like Your people are not experiencing Your protection and Your blessing? Lord, I can't go on until I have an answer from You." I felt like if God wasn't protecting others, then how could I trust Him to protect me?

I had an internal confidence that He would answer me. For two or three days I waited on God. As I was driving in my SUV soon thereafter, the Holy Spirit spoke to me deep within my heart: "The reason you are seeing My people failing and falling is because they are not trusting Me." This was spoken to me with such clarity and depth of revelation that I knew it was a *rhema* word (a personal word from God) to me.

I knew that He was talking about more than just trust, as I previously understood it. He showed me that He wanted His people to *cling* to Him. At that moment I learned that trusting actually is clinging. "They're not clinging to Me," He said. "They're not holding on to Me."

I immediately thought about the words of Jesus, *"Blessed are the poor in spirit, for theirs is the kingdom of heaven"* (Matt. 5:3). To me, being poor in spirit speaks of dependency on the Lord. When we're not walking in dependency upon the Lord, but are living according to our own ways, we are going to fail and fall. We will also be putting ourselves in a position where we are vulnerable to the enemy's attack.

Please understand that God is often protecting His people even when they are not clinging to Him. However, in order to see His manifest blessing as recorded in Psalm 91, we must draw near to Him. As we learn to cling to the Lord, we will experience His favor, victory, and blessing more fully.

Sometimes God lets us fall on our faces in order to break us to bring us into a fuller experience in Him. For example, I've talked to many people who have had health challenges and have testified that going through their physical challenge made them more dependent on God. As a result of this, their relationship with Him is much closer now. God does indeed cause "all things to work together for good to those who are called according to His purpose" (Rom. 8:28).

TRUSTING GOD FOR OURSELVES

The devil will sometimes distract God's people from a general truth with what appears to be an exception. He does this to keep us from receiving the revelation of God's love. Satan does not want us to receive and believe the simple truth of God's Word. He loves to sidetrack us with examples that seem to contradict the Word of God. In other words, we can see a person who names the name of Jesus fall into tremendous hardships and we're tempted to wonder whether we can trust God. We think to ourselves, "Well, God didn't seem to bless and protect them, so I wonder if I can trust Him."

When a believer is tragically killed or dies suddenly, Satan will often try to arouse doubt in believers' minds: "Can God really be trusted? Why did that individual die?" I've found a wonderful verse that addresses this situation: Isaiah 57:1-2. Isaiah says, *The righteous man perishes, and no man takes it to heart; and devout men are taken away, while no one understands. For the righteous man is taken away from evil, he enters into peace.* God takes righteous people from the earth in order to keep them from evil, to bless them, and to bring them into rest.

Some things fall into the realm of mystery, and I certainly don't have answers to everything. When we're confronted with troubling scenarios that we don't understand, we need to declare with the psalmist: *"O Lord, my heart is not proud, nor my eyes haughty; nor do I involve myself in great matters, or things too difficult for me"* (Ps. 131:1). The psalmist was saying here that he wasn't going to concern himself with trying to figure everything out. Instead, he humbly trusted God and His goodness.

Satan tries to keep us trapped by attempting to have us measure God's faithfulness by looking at other people and their situations. But we have to trust God and cling to Him for ourselves instead of trying to trust Him based on the experiences of others. I should not determine if I can trust God based on whether I think He was faithful to somebody else. I need to trust Him for myself. My confidence in God must be based upon His Word alone. I once heard a man say, "When you don't understand God's ways, trust in God's heart."

LET'S BELIEVE

Let's believe, beloved, that God is always with us. He will never leave us nor forsake us. He is with us every moment of every day, even until the end of the world.

Let's believe, beloved, that God is our shield and He is protecting us.

Let's believe, beloved, that no evil will befall us or our children.

Let's believe, beloved, that God will lead our children to marry the right mates.

Let's believe, beloved, that God will watch over our finances and give us good health.

Let's believe, beloved, that God will protect us on the road.

Let's believe, beloved, that God will be with us in our old age.

Let's believe, beloved, that the Lord will sustain us in every area and at every time of life.

Let's believe, beloved, that God's loving-kindness will be with us always.

Let's believe, beloved, with the apostle Paul: *"For I am convinced that neither death, nor life, nor angels, nor principalities, nor things present, nor things to come, nor powers, nor height, nor depth, nor any other created thing, will be able to separate us from the love of God, which is in Christ Jesus our Lord"* (Rom. 8:38-39).

Prayer: Father, I choose to believe Your Word, which is truth. I thank You that Your truth is setting me free. I cling to You now in total faith that You do all things well, and I believe that all things work together for good in my life. Instead of worrying, I will trust You. Instead of fretting, I will abide in You. Instead of fearing, I will walk in Your love. Instead of being anxious, I will pray and cast all my cares upon You. I love You, Father God, and I know that You are with me always. By Your grace, I will not fear any longer. Thank You for all the promises of Your Word. In Jesus's name.

7

APPLYING GOD'S WORD

For the Word of God is living and active and
sharper than any two-edged sword, and piercing
as far as the division of soul and spirit, of both
joints and marrow, and able to judge the thoughts
and intentions of the heart (Hebrews 4:12).

FAITH COMES BY HEARING GOD'S WORD

We must really believe that we can be free from the fears that plague us. God has provided a glorious liberty for His children: *"The creation itself also will be set free from its slavery to corruption into the freedom of the glory of the children of God"* (Rom. 8:21). Christ has set us free from corruption and fear, and we are now able to enjoy the freedom of the glory Jesus provided for us.

Paul says that *"faith comes from hearing, and hearing by the word of Christ"* (Rom. 10:17). We need to immerse ourselves in the Word of God to develop faith, for faith comes through the Word of God. There are, of course, many ways we can *receive* God's Word—we can read it, memorize it, and meditate upon it. But one of the ways we get it into our spirits is through saturating ourselves by praying it.

By praying God's Word, we are expressing faith back to God. By praying His Word, we continually grow in our intimacy with Him, and His ways become ours. Our outlook on life will be transformed.

In order to pray God's Word effectively, we must learn to personalize it—to make it our own. Here is an example that will help us understand how to do this on a practical level. Since Joshua 1:9 has been important to us throughout the book, we'll turn it into prayer before the Lord.

> **Prayer:** *Father, I thank You for your commandment to be strong and courageous! Through Your grace and with Your help, I will not tremble or be dismayed. I ask You to lift this burden of fear from my life, and to set me completely free. I believe You are doing this. And I thank You for your love, mercy, and grace, which enable me to walk in freedom from all fear. Thank You for being with me wherever I go. This knowledge brings great peace to me. In Jesus's name I pray, amen.*

This is just one example of how we turn Joshua 1:9 into a personal prayer. There is more than one way to do this. Turn God's Word into your own personal prayers as you pray His Word back to Him. His Word has the power to create faith within us. As we personalize it and turn it into prayer, our faith will increase.

JESUS HAD NO FEAR

Nowhere in the Gospels does Jesus express fear in any way. And the same Jesus who walked the earth two thousand years ago now lives inside of each of us, so His fearlessness dwells inside of us. Beloved, this is a wonderful truth that is worthy of our meditation. The One who knew no fear, the One who had all authority in heaven and on earth, lives within you and me.

Do you remember the time when Jesus's disciples were facing fear while they were on a boat in the middle of the Sea of Galilee? The Bible describes it this way:

> *Leaving the crowd, they took Him along with them in the boat, just as He was; and other boats were with Him. And there arose a fierce gale of wind, and the waves were breaking over the boat so much that the boat was already filling up. Jesus Himself was in the stern, asleep on the cushion; and they woke Him and said to Him, "Teacher, do You not care that we are perishing?" And He got up and rebuked the wind and said to the sea, "Hush, be still." And the wind died down and it became perfectly calm. And He said to them, "Why are you afraid? How is it that you have no faith?" They became very much afraid and said to one another, "Who then is this, that even the wind and the sea obey Him?"* (Mark 4:36-41)

The disciples were understandably afraid of the situation. Their fear was real; it was not simply a figment of their imaginations. They asked the Master for help, and He helped. We must do the same whenever we are afraid in the circumstances that surround our lives.

When Jesus woke up on the boat that was being tossed about on the raging waves, He first rebuked the storm, then He rebuked the disciples for their lack of faith in the midst of the storm. He first revealed His power to them; then He told them that the answer to their fear was faith.

If we are going to keep ourselves from being afraid and experience a new energy, confidence, and a fresh fire within, we must find a way to increase our faith. Our faith is going to increase as we pray back to God

His transforming Word. The more our faith increases, the more we will know that God is present.

SEIZING GOD'S WORD

Beloved, Jesus cleanses us from all sin through the power of His Word. So we must seize His Word and let it do its mighty work within us. We can strengthen ourselves through consistently reading, meditating on, and praying the Word of God back to Him. His Word has strengthening and cleaning powers: *"You are already clean because of the word which I have spoken unto you"* (John 15:3).

We must also have faith in the truth and validity of God's Word if it is to make a great impact upon us. We need to really believe that He loves us with a love that is unconditional, a love that is incorruptible, and a love that is eternal. We learn in the Word of God that He is fighting for us, He knows everything we're going through, He is involved in our lives, and He is always present with us.

I remember a time not long ago when the Lord awoke me in the middle of the night. It was a powerful encounter with Him, where He said to me, "Seize My Word, and don't let anything else in." I have treasured that word ever since. That word is also for you, beloved.

The Lord's commandment to "Be strong" (see Joshua 1:9) entails hardening and fortifying ourselves against all the works of the enemy. This is faith in action, and only a warring faith works. If we're not in warfare mode, if we are not actively seeking God, if we are not choosing to believe God, if we are not strengthening ourselves in the Word of God consistently, we are vulnerable to fear's attack.

We must be ever vigilant in this area of our lives. Peter wrote, *"Be of sober spirit, be on the alert. Your adversary, the devil, prowls around like a roaring lion, seeking someone to devour. But resist him, firm in your faith, knowing that the same experiences of suffering are being accomplished by your brethren who are in the world"* (1 Pet. 5:8-9).

DEFEATING FEAR THROUGH GOD'S WORD

I want us to now look at three important weapons by which, when properly used, will defeat fear in our lives.

Knowing God Is with Us

Knowing God is with us is a spiritual weapon, which is the shield of faith, that can be used very effectively against the enemy. We can actually say to him, "Get away from me, Satan, for my God is with me. He will never leave me nor forsake me. He is always with me, even unto the end of the age."

Psalm 23 reminds us of God's dwelling with us through the midst of every circumstance we may go through in life—both good and bad. David declared, *"Even though I walk through the valley of the shadow of death, I fear no evil, for You are with me"* (vs. 4). David knew God was with him so he was not afraid to pass through the valley of the shadow of death. And in Psalm 118 we read, *"The Lord is with me; I will not be afraid. What can man do to me?"* (vs. 6 NIV).

Likewise, in Deuteronomy 31:6 we read, *"Be strong and courageous, do not be afraid or tremble at them, for the Lord your God is the one who goes with you. He will not fail you or forsake you."* Beloved, do you see how important it is to know that the Lord is with you at all times? If we really know this in our heart of hearts, then we will no longer have to deal with fear on a continual basis.

We must remember that we are not alone in this world, even if there are no other people around us. We are not orphans; God has adopted us into His spiritual family. He has chosen us from the foundation of the world to be united with Him, to be one with Him.

Using God's Word

God's Word is sharper than any two-edged sword (Heb. 4:12). It is our offensive weapon against the enemy's wiles, schemes, and devices (Eph.

6:17). His Word is the sword of the Spirit, and it will cause the devil to flee, just as he did when Jesus quoted from God's Word in the wilderness.

When the devil told Jesus to tell the stone to become bread, He replied, *"It is written, 'Man shall not live on bread alone.'"* When the devil asked Jesus to worship him, the Lord said, *"It is written, 'You shall worship the Lord your God and serve Him only."* It was then that the devil used Scripture for his own devices and said, *"If You are the Son of God, throw Yourself down from here; for it is written, 'He will command His angels concerning you to guard you,' and, 'On their hands they will bear you up, so that You will not strike Your foot against a stone.'"* Jesus answered, *"It is said, 'You shall not put the Lord your God to the test'"* (Luke 4:1-12).

Jesus's use of the Word in His encounter with the devil was effective. Luke records, *"When the devil had finished every temptation, he left Him until an opportune time"* (Luke 4:13). If we are walking in the Word and using it as our spiritual sword to fight our battles, we will be empowered to deal with the enemy's attacks. Like Jesus, we will defeat him by using God's Word as a sword against him.

Believing with Our Heart

If we are to overcome the assaults of the enemy, then we must walk in the faith and trust that come from God's Word. The psalmist made the connection between faith in God and the assimilation of His Word when he wrote, *"When I am afraid, I will put my trust in You. In God, whose Word I praise, in God I have put my trust; I shall not be afraid. What can mere man do to me?"* (Ps. 56:3-4).

Faith is the victory that overcomes the world. Hebrews 11, the great faith chapter of the New Testament, says that it was through faith that Abel, Enoch, Noah, Abraham, Sarah, and so many others prevailed over their circumstances (Heb. 11:33-35). These men and women were able to do great things without fear because they expressed faith in God's Word in His promises.

As we walk in faith, we will be able to look fear in the face with the absolute assurance that *"God causes all things to work together for good to those who love God, to those who are called according to His purpose"* (Rom. 8:28). We are to exercise faith in the supernatural acts of God and believe that He will always do what He says He will do throughout His Word.

The prophet Isaiah assures us:

> But now, thus says the Lord, your Creator, O Jacob, and He who formed you, O Israel, "Do not fear, for I have redeemed you; I have called you by name; you are Mine! When you pass through the waters, I will be with you; and through the rivers, they will not overflow you. When you walk through the fire, you will not be scorched, nor will the flame burn you. For I am the Lord your God, the Holy One of Israel, your Savior; I have given Egypt as your ransom, Cush and Seba in your place. Since you are precious in My sight, since you are honored and I love you.... Do not fear, for I am with you" (Isaiah 43:1-5).

FALSE MENTAL IMAGES

Satan is adept at putting false mental pictures in people's minds—images of all kinds of imagined happenings that are designed to arouse fear in our hearts. Don't believe these images even for a second. Regardless of what we go through, God is with us.

You see, God's sacred name, Yahweh, is a verb that shows continuous, unfinished action. I'm sure most of us have never thought of God as a verb—an active force that is at work in our lives. But the truth is that He is involved in our lives, at every level. He cares so deeply about everything that affects us. He's involved in all our circumstances, even when things look dim and hope is obscure.

Hebrews defines faith as *"the assurance of things hoped for, the conviction of things not seen"* (Heb. 11:1). We do not have to fear what the world fears. The only thing we want to fear is God.

A TESTIMONY: FREE FROM FEAR

I have two beautiful daughters, and within one month they both had serious car accidents. As a result of this, fear re-entered my life. Satan found a chink in my armor. He put all kinds of false mental images in my mind that truly scared me. Every time one of my daughters walked out the door to get into their car, I was overwhelmed with the fear of them getting into an accident.

One afternoon during this time, I felt so overwhelmed and defeated by these fears that assailed me, that I took a nap to escape them. While I was sleeping, I found myself dreaming that I was crying out to our congregation, "Pray for me; I need your help."

When I awoke, I went downstairs and checked my phone. There was a message from someone in our congregation who had only called me two or three times in the last few years. "Rabbi, I started praying a while ago, and, as I did so, the Lord put your face right in front of me. Rabbi, I don't know what your need is, but I'm praying for you."

Her call had come during my naptime when I was dreaming and calling out to my congregation for help and asking for their prayers. God cared enough to put my face in front of this woman as she prayed that day. He heard and answered my prayer for deliverance from fear while I was fast asleep.

As she prayed for me over the phone, I felt free from the fear that had been tormenting me for so long. God had intervened in my situation and set me free from the fear that was trying to torment me. God is with us; He hears our prayers and He wants to set us free from fear. Beloved, the Lord is faithful to all of His promises contained in His Word; He will never let us down. As we continue to turn His promises back to Him through prayer, He will continue to strengthen us in our fight against fear.

Prayer: *Heavenly Father, I know You love me and know the number of the hairs on my head. I know You do not want me to be afraid. I bless You today, Yeshua. Help me trust in Your love, to believe that You are with me always, and to take my stand upon Your Word. As I do so, I pray I would experience Your perfect peace that surpasses all understanding. Through faith in Your Word, I know I shall prevail. In the blessed name of Yeshua I pray, amen.*

8

GOD IS BIGGER THAN OUR FEAR

When I am afraid, I will put my trust in You. In God, whose word I praise, in God I have put my trust; I shall not be afraid (Psalm 56:3-4).

TEN TRUTHS TO KNOW

David asked, *"How can a young man keep his way pure?"* Then he immediately answers, *"By keeping it according to Your word"* (Ps. 119:9). And then he further says, *"Your word have I treasured in my heart, that I might not sin against You"* (Ps. 119:11). I want to explain ten truths God wants us to know from His Word regarding fear and faith. This is so we can treasure His Truth in our hearts, in order to be empowered in our fight against fear. God is always bigger than our fear.

1. Do Not Be Afraid

The title of this book, *Do Not Be Afraid!*, is taken directly from Luke 12:32: *"Do not be afraid, little flock, for your Father has chosen gladly to give you the kingdom"* (Luke 12:32). This commandment to not fear is given more than a hundred times throughout the Scriptures.

Jesus' words seem so tender here. He is not rebuking us because we fear, but rather reassures us because He understands we have real fears. There is something about His voice that arrests our attention and causes us to take notice of what He is about to say. When He speaks, it is imperative that we believe and obey what He says.

As we follow the Lord, we can know with full certainty that nothing will be able to snatch us away from Him. David wrote,

> *The Lord is my shepherd, I shall not want. He makes me lie down in green pastures; He leads me beside quiet waters. He restores my soul; He guides me in the paths of righteousness for His name's sake. Even though I walk through the valley of the shadow of death, I fear no evil, for You are with me* (Psalm 23:1-4).

A shepherd takes good care of his sheep. He makes sure they have plenty to eat, are well watered, and that nothing harms them. He continually guides them and guards them, endeavoring to keep them safe. Beloved, this is what God promises to do for us. Because God cares for us more than a shepherd does his sheep, we don't have to fear any longer, for He leads us through life.

2. *God Cares for Us*

Peter writes, *"Therefore humble yourselves under the mighty hand of God, that He may exalt you at the proper time, casting all your anxiety upon Him, because He cares for you"* (1 Pet. 5:6-7). Beloved, God loves us with an everlasting love, and He cares about us and everything that affects us. He does not want us to fear anyone or anything. He knows all about us, the number of hairs on our head and the number of days of our lifetime. He knows us, loves us, and wants us to lean into Him.

The psalmist declared, *"Blessed be the Lord, who daily bears our burden, the God who is our salvation"* (Ps. 68:19). Yes, God is the great burden-bearer, and Jesus said in the same manner, *"Come to Me, all who are weary and heavy-laden, and I will give you rest. Take My yoke upon you and learn from Me, for I am gentle and humble in heart, and you will find rest for your souls. For My yoke is easy and My burden is light"* (Matt. 11:28-30). We are to yoke ourselves to Jesus, remembering that He loves us and will always work on our behalf. He knows us and wants us to lean into Him.

These promises from God's Word bring peace and rest to our souls, which keep us from being afraid. The truth is that God has already given us every spiritual blessing in Christ Jesus (Eph. 1:3), including the ability to overcome fear. This is a part of our inheritance.

3. Jesus Gives Us Peace

Before Jesus departed back to the Father, He said, *"Peace I leave with you; My peace I give to you; not as the world gives do I give to you. Do not let your heart be troubled, nor let it be fearful"* (John 14:27). One of the many gifts that Jesus has imparted to us is His perfect, incomparable peace—a peace that surpasses all understanding.

In the same way that there is no fear in heaven, there can be no fear in Jesus's peace. We are to walk in peace, for Isaiah said of God, *"The steadfast of mind You will keep in perfect peace, because he trusts in You"* (Isa. 26:3). Faith keeps our mind steadfast before the Lord, in a state of peace.

4. No Weapon Formed Against Us Will Prosper

Isaiah assures us of this: *"'No weapon that is formed against you will prosper; and every tongue that accuses you in judgment you will condemn. This is the heritage of the servants of the Lord. And their vindication is from Me,' says the Lord"* (Isa. 54:17). Satan has a lot of weapons to use in his attack against us, but none of them will prosper in their attempt to destroy us.

Satan's plans won't prosper because Jesus has triumphed over our enemy.

5. *There Is No Condemnation*

Paul wrote to the Romans, *"Therefore there is now no condemnation for those who are in Christ Jesus. For the law of the Spirit of life in Christ Jesus has set you free from the law of sin and death"* (Rom. 8:1-2).

Adam felt condemned after he ate fruit from the tree of the knowledge of good and evil, and condemnation and shame have haunted the human race ever since. Feeling condemned makes us afraid. After Adam ate from the tree he felt condemned and began to run in fear. The first words out of his mouth after eating from the forbidden tree were *"I was afraid"* (Gen. 3:10). But the Bible says there is now no condemnation for those who are in Christ Jesus. All condemnation and guilt have been washed away by the blood of Yeshua—He took them upon Himself on the cross. There is to be no condemnation and no fear. *"It was for freedom that Christ set us free; therefore keep standing firm and do not be subject again to a yoke of slavery"* (Gal. 5:1).

6. *We Have Been Adopted into God's Family*

Romans 8:15 says, *"For you have not received a spirit of slavery leading to fear again, but you have received a spirit of adoption as sons by which we cry out, 'Abba, Father!'"* The word *abba* is an Aramaic term that may be interpreted literally as "daddy." As our daddy, He wants only the best for us; His desire is for us to live a life that is free from fear, worry, and torment.

Even earthly fathers want to provide peace, security, happiness, and protection for their children. Jesus compared earthly fathers with the heavenly Father in this respect:

> *For everyone who asks receives, and he who seeks finds, and to him who knocks it will be opened. Or what man is there among you who, when his son asks for a loaf, will give him a*

stone? Or if he asks for a fish, he will not give him a snake, will he? If you then, being evil, know how to give good gifts to your children, how much more will your Father who is in heaven give what is good to those who ask Him!" (Matthew 7:8-11)

Abba has adopted us into His family, and that means we are entitled to enjoy everything our Father has for us: *"Every good thing given and every perfect gift is from above, coming down from the Father of lights, with whom there is no variation or shifting shadow"* (James 1:17). One of these perfect gifts that Father wants us, His children, to have is freedom from fear.

7. All Things Work Together for Good

Beloved, God has called us according to His purpose, and He will always do whatever is necessary to make sure that His purposes are fulfilled in our life. Paul assured us of this when he said, *"And we know that God causes all things to work together for good to those who love God, to those who are called according to His purpose"* (Rom. 8:28).

His promise to you and me is, *"I will visit you and fulfill My good word to you…. For I know the plans that I have for you…to give you a future and a hope"* (Jer. 29:10-11). God's plans will surely be fulfilled in our lives. We do not need to worry about the future, for the future is in His hands. Because we trust that He is sovereign, we can be assured that all things will work together for good in our lives.

8. God Extends His Hand to Us

God promises, *"For I am the Lord, your God, who takes hold of your right hand, who says to you, 'Do not fear, I will help you'"* (Isa. 41:13). *"I am the Lord, I have called You in righteousness, I will also hold You by the hand and watch over You"* (Isa. 42:6). *"When he falls, he will not be hurled headlong, because the Lord is the One who holds his hand"* (Ps. 37:24). God never lets His Word return to Him void. He promises to help us, and we can count on it in the midst of trouble.

We have no reason to ever be afraid because God is holding our hand. Imagine God taking hold of our right hand, lifting us up, and leading us through the darkest situation we can imagine. We can listen to His voice saying, "Don't fear, my beloved child, I am with you to help you." By faith we simply take hold of His hand and let Him lead us each step of the way.

9. God Has Not Given Us Fear

The attributes of the spirit God gave us are love, power, and self-control. Paul told Timothy, *"For God has not given us a spirit of timidity, but of power and love and discipline"* (2 Tim. 1:7). That means we no longer need to be cowardly; we no longer need to be intimidated by anyone or anything. Our spirit is filled with love, power, and discipline, which all comes from the Lord.

And Paul says, *"Finally, be strong in the Lord and in the strength of His might"* (Eph. 6:10). The power we need to fight against fear comes from being strong in the Lord and remembering that He will fight for us. We are to stand strong in the Lord, letting Him fight our battles. So don't be timid, but launch out with full faith in God's Word.

10. There Is No Fear in Love

John writes, *"There is no fear in love; but perfect love casts out fear, because fear involves punishment, and the one who fears is not perfected in love"* (1 John 4:18). We are to allow His love to have full sway in our life so that we will be able to be perfected in Him. *"The love of God has been poured out within our hearts through the Holy Spirit who was given to us"* (Rom. 5:5). We need to choose love.

As we walk in the love of God, fear will have a hard time finding roots in our hearts. The same love that dwells in us is the very same love that motivated the Father in giving us Jesus: *"For God so loved the world, that He gave His only begotten Son, that whosoever believes in Him shall not perish, but have eternal life"* (John 3:16).

It is clear throughout the Scriptures that God wants us to rise above all fear and be completely free from its grip. The time to enter into this living reality is now. But in our fight against fear, it's important to remember that it is all about God, and His love.

> **Prayer:** *Father, I ask that You would release Your power within me. Help me to have faith in the truth of Your Word. Father, I thank You for Your Word, which is the Word of truth. I thank You for Jesus, who is the way, the truth, and the life. And I thank You for the Holy Spirit, who is the Spirit of truth. I'm so grateful You are at work in my life, giving me the power and revelation I need to break off fear from my life.*

GOD IS FIGHTING FOR US

Since it is the truth that sets us free, we must have faith in that truth (John 8:32). We are to believe that God, who is bigger than our fear, is fighting for us. He is with us and He goes before us. When we are afraid, it's because we don't really believe that God is involved in our life. This needs to change, beloved.

> *Indeed, the very hairs of your head are all numbered. Do not fear; you are more valuable than many sparrows* (Luke 12:7)

We believe that when we get to heaven, everything will be all right, but we sometimes lack the faith to realize that He yearns to be involved in the day-to-day details of our earthly life as well.

COURAGE IN THE MIDST OF FEAR

There is a story about Jesus that I love found in Mark 6:45-52. In the evening time, the disciples were paddling hard in the middle of the sea going nowhere. Jesus came up to them, walking on the sea, and they cried out in fear because they thought He was a ghost. *"But immediately He spoke with them and said to them, 'Take courage; it is I, do not be afraid.' Then He got into the boat with them, and the wind stopped; and they were utterly astonished"* (Mark 6:50-51). Notice in this story that Yeshua commands them to take courage and not to be afraid. A similar incident, again dealing with the themes of courage, fear and doubt, takes place in Matthew 14:27-33.

> *But immediately Jesus spoke to them, saying, "Take courage, it is I; do not be afraid." Peter said to Him, "Lord, if it is You, command me to come to You on the water." And He said, "Come!" And Peter got out of the boat, and walked on the water and came toward Jesus. But seeing the wind, he became frightened, and beginning to sink, he cried out, "Lord, save me!" Immediately Jesus stretched out His hand and took hold of him, and said to him, "You of little faith, why did you doubt?" When they got into the boat, the wind stopped. And those who were in the boat worshiped Him, saying, "You are certainly God's Son!"* (Matthew 14:27-33)

Why was Jesus so concerned about Peter's lack of faith? It's because He knows faith is what we need to keep us from falling, and to stop being afraid. The courage we need comes from faith, and faith comes from getting into God's Word and spending time with the Lord. When Peter looked at the wind instead of Jesus, he began to sink. He would have drowned had not Jesus been there to save him. The same thing happens to us when we're not trusting God, seizing His Word, and spending time with Him. We begin to sink under the circumstances of our life.

In this passage of scripture that we just read, we see that doubt is related to fear. Doubting God's Word, doubting God's presence, and doubting His character robs us of victory. Jesus said to Peter, *"You of little faith, why did you doubt?"* (Matt. 14:31).

Sometimes this downward spiral begins with just a thought: "Can I really trust God?" This question then leads to doubt and doubt leads to fear. Always remember that faith is the channel through which God moves, and fear is the channel through which Satan moves.

A high-wire artist in a circus is trained to never look down as he walks along the tightrope, for if he looks down, he will begin to grow afraid and fall. He will lose his balance because his focus is on the wrong thing. This is what happened to Peter, and it's what happens to us when we get our eyes off of Jesus. When we have our eyes fixed on Jesus, we are victorious; but when our eyes are on the things of the world, we begin to falter.

There have been times I've called directory assistance in order to get a phone number, but I didn't have a pen or paper with me to write down the number the operator (or recorded voice) gave me. The times when I feared I would not be able to remember the number, doubt robbed me and I could not remember it. The same thing happens when an athlete thinks he is not going to catch a ball or be able to break through the line. His doubt engenders fear, and thus he fails.

We do not need to fear or be thrown off balance. We do not need to be influenced by evil or the world of darkness. We must use faith and visualize ourselves being successful in overcoming difficult circumstances if we are to be successful in this fight against fear. We must continually speak God's words to our mind and heart. We are to believe; take courage. Whether it involves something at work, our health, our finances, a relationship, an athletic competition, a public speaking engagement, playing an instrument, or something else entirely, we are to stand confidently upon the Lord's Word and look to Jesus. God is much bigger than our fears.

Prayer: *Father, I come to Your throne to receive grace and mercy in my time of need. I believe Your Word, and I know I shall prevail. In fact, I am more than a conqueror through Him who gives me strength. Thank You, Jesus, for always being with me and helping me overcome my fear. I know that You are bigger than any fear I face. In Messiah Jesus's name. Amen.*

9

NO FEAR: BEING DIFFERENT FROM THE WORLD

Do not grieve the Holy Spirit of God, by whom you were
sealed for the day of redemption (Ephesians 4:30).

A CONGREGATION OF THE LORD

On Valentine's Day 2007, the congregation I lead, Adat Adonai World Outreach Center (now called Lion of Judah World Outreach Center), began a 24-hour prayer room that we call the Key of David. Three months after we opened the prayer room, I received a call from the pastor who owned the building we were meeting in at the time. He said, "Rabbi, I regret to inform you that the building has been sold, and you will have to move out in thirty days."

Feeling blindsided by his words, I went to the Lord and prayed, "I have waited on You for inner transformation, and, as a result, I have more peace, power, and authority in my life than ever before. It's tangible and real. Just as I've waited on You for inner transformation and You anchored me and changed me on the inside, now I'm going to wait on You to see You act in my outer world."

I refused to let fear, panic, or worry enter into my heart. My natural tendency would have been to rush around and look for a new building immediately, but I knew that was not God's way. Instead, He wanted me to trust Him and wait for Him in this situation for a period of two weeks.

Even though our congregation had been in existence for eighteen years, we had never owned our own building. The time had come for God to give us a building, so I felt comfortable about waiting for Him to move. So three days after receiving the call, I told the congregation about our predicament, and how the Lord had instructed me to do nothing but wait upon Him until May 14th, which was a period of two weeks. After the service, people came up to me with great anxiety because of the situation. I told them, "I'm just going to wait on the Lord."

When two weeks were up, we still didn't have a building, and now we had only two remaining weeks to move out of our present building. To be honest, my faith began to shrink a little at this point. I wondered, "Have I been totally irresponsible? How many pastors would have left their congregation in this type of predicament? What kind of leader am I? I should have been planning for this a couple of years ago!"

A Profound Dream

However, that night I had a dream where I was crying out to God due to the excruciating pain I was experiencing, feeling as if God had abandoned me. "I trusted You in this," I cried. "I told Your people that You supernaturally led us into this building, and that You would supernaturally lead us to the next place when it was time. I obeyed You and waited upon You. Now here I am with no place to go."

All of a sudden, a golden spear (approximately two feet long and one inch wide) appeared in my dream that pierced right through my forehead and came out through the back of my neck. It was then that I sensed God's Spirit speaking to me, "You have obeyed Me to the end in this. You didn't panic, and you trusted Me. You didn't take matters into your own hands or act on your own initiative; you waited on Me. Now

I've slain you with My truth, and it is now your possession. You will be able to live the rest of your life waiting upon Me, seeing Me go before you, doing the work."

When I awoke from the dream, I felt greatly encouraged even though I still didn't know where the Lord would take our congregation. After calling many pastors in our area to see if they would allow us to meet in their buildings, a pastor finally invited us to share their sanctuary until we found our own place to buy. I had found an answer, although a temporary one, to our dilemma.

A Prophetic Word

Within a few days, a member of our congregation—a soft-spoken lady not known for giving prophetic words—called me with a prophetic word she had received in our prayer room. "The Lord says, 'I gave you May 14, and now I give you June 14. On June 14 you will have your building." Her words were encouraging.

A realtor took me to see an old Veterans of Foreign Wars (VFW) hall in Toledo's inner city. It seemed to be the only available property that was large enough for our congregation, and within our budget. It would mean, however, that our congregation would have to move from the suburbs to the inner city.

I gave the realtor an offer for the building, and the trustees of the building said they would present the offer to their general membership for a vote "a week from Thursday." When I looked at my calendar, I realized that "a week from Thursday" was June 14, confirmation of the prophetic word I had received earlier. On Thursday, June 14, the realtor called me to let me know that the VFW had accepted our offer. Because I was ecstatic about this news, I went before the congregation with the blowing of shofars, declaring to the congregation that God had arisen and proven Himself faithful.

Though the devil had tempted me to worry about this, I did not listen to his lies. I waited on God and He came through, just as He always does when we are obedient to Him. I prayed, "God, You're so faithful! I trust You! You love me so much, and I thank You that Your favor is upon me. This is so incredible!"

A few days after I prayed this prayer, the phone rang with the architect on the other line. He wanted to let me know that many things would have to be done to the building in order to bring it up to code. He estimated the cost of these renovations to be between $150,000 and $200,000. Now this money wasn't for remodeling the building, which it also needed, but it was just to bring it up to code.

My high had now turned into a low with one phone call. How could we, as a congregation, afford this? I cried out to the Lord, "What's going on here? Did You set me up just to humiliate me and expose me as a false prophet? My ministry is over. No one will ever have confidence in me again."

Fear was hitting me now full force. As I was driving to our temporary meeting place the next day, I began to think and pray, "Lord, there must be one of three things going on here: either You set me up to humiliate me because You don't want me to lead this congregation any longer; or somehow You're going to have these code requirements waived; or You'll miraculously provide us with the money we need."

My faith was fighting the fear, and I went into the prayer room to seek the Lord for the entire day. While in the prayer room, I considered a fourth option, maybe God had orchestrated everything to take us out of the market until the right property became available.

An Appointment with Destiny

The next day as I was driving into the parking lot, I noticed a lady I had never seen before standing there. She asked me, "Is there someone I can talk to who is in authority over Adat Adonai?" She had seen the sign in front of the church advertising it as our temporary home.

She explained that she was a realtor and had just received a listing she thought would be just right for our congregation. So I went with her to see the property right away. It was on several acres in a beautiful suburban neighborhood in Ottawa Lake, Michigan, just outside of Toledo. And it was close to an area that was populated by Jewish people.

The Lord had led us to the property that was just right for us. We bought it, and we closed the sale on the exact same day we had been scheduled to close on the first building. The building God blessed us with was beautiful. I thank God that I did not take this matter into my own hands, fretting and trying to do things in my own wisdom and strength. (We have since relocated to a larger building in Toledo, Ohio.)

No matter what we are going through, God will take care of it—He did it for us and He will do it for you. The Father wants to prove Himself faithful in our lives. When we trust Him to do the work, He will accomplish great things.

THREE TRUTHS TO REMEMBER

To fight fear in our life effectively, we must keep the following three truths in mind:

1. *The devil is our enemy, and fear is his biggest weapon.*

How can we be successful in our warfare against him? We must put on the whole armor of God. Paul instructs us:

> *Finally, be strong in the Lord and in the strength of His might. Put on the full armor of God, so that you will be able to stand firm against the schemes of the devil. For our struggle is not against flesh and blood, but against the rulers, against the powers, against the world forces of this darkness, against the spiritual forces of wickedness in the heavenly places. Therefore, take up the full armor of God, so that you will be able to resist in the evil day, and having done everything, to stand firm. Stand firm therefore, having girded your loins with truth, and having put on the breastplate of righteousness, and having shod your feet with the preparation of the gospel of peace, in addition to all, taking up the*

shield of faith with which you will be able to extinguish all the flaming arrows of the evil one. And take the helmet of salvation, and the sword of the Spirit, which is the word of God (Ephesians 6:10-17).

2. God wants to strengthen us.

To be strengthened means that we are hardened for the fight. The Hebrew word for this is *amatz*. God wants to teach us how to steel ourselves for the warfare that rages all around us. We need to harden ourselves toward Satan's lies, making sure the door of our heart is firmly locked against him. We need to pray that God will strengthen us with His divine fire (*aish*), divine electricity, and divine power. We need His *aish* to rise up within us as we declare war on fear.

As we learn to lean on God, clinging to Him in faith and trust, He will take us from strength to strength and from glory to glory. We can pray with the psalmist, *"Strengthen me according to Your Word"* (Ps. 119:28).

Prayer: *Father, You said in Your Word that we would be able to take the kingdom of God by force, and this is what I want to do. Help me to be violent against Satan. I want to go all the way with You, Father. Help me to overcome and topple all fear. Thank You for Your promise that I will be able to tread upon all the power of the enemy and upon snakes and scorpions. I pray that I wouldn't be passive, Father, but be active in this warfare, realizing how serious it is. Though Your grace I will close the door of my heart to fear. Strengthen me, O Father God. In the name of Yeshua I pray, amen.*

3. We bow down only to God.

The only one we should fear is God Himself, and fear, in this context, means we are to worship, adore, and respect Him with reverence.

Yeshua said, *"But an hour is coming, and now is, when the true worshipers will worship the Father in spirit and truth; for such people the Father seeks to be His worshipers. God is spirit, and those who worship Him must worship in spirit and truth"* (John 4:23-24).

God wants our worship, desires it, and He alone deserves it. Faith always bows down to God through worship, but fear bows down to the devil. When we bow down to fear, we are not worshiping God but the enemy. Faith affirms that God is with us and loves us. Fear denies Him.

I pray that we will learn to worship the Lord in the beauty of holiness standing against fear!

DIFFERENT FROM OTHERS

Peter wrote, *"But you are a chosen race, a royal priesthood, a holy nation, a people for God's own possession, so that you may proclaim the excellencies of Him who has called you out of darkness into His marvelous light"* (1 Pet. 2:9). Because we have been called out of darkness and into God's marvelous light, we are a part of His royal priesthood. This means we are to walk circumspectly and avoid being like the other people in the world.

We have been called out of the world, and we're not to resemble it in any way. Yes, we live in the world, but we're not to be of this word—we're also citizens of heaven. We are not to walk according to the ways of this world, but be transformed by letting our minds be renewed. Paul said,

> *Therefore I urge you, brethren, by the mercies of God, to present your bodies a living and holy sacrifice, acceptable to God, which is your spiritual service of worship. And do not be conformed to this world, but be transformed by the renewing of your mind, so that you may prove what the will of God is, that which is good and acceptable and perfect* (Romans 12:1-2).

Though others around us are terrified and talking about the economy collapsing, the government being corrupt, the horrors of terrorism, nuclear threats, and all kinds of disasters, we are not to be like them—we are not to walk in fear but in faith. We are to remain in God's peace and rest. The world's negativity cannot be allowed to affect us.

> *You are not to say, "It is a conspiracy!" In regard to all that this people call a conspiracy, and you are not to fear what they fear or be in dread of it. It is the Lord of hosts whom you should regard as holy. And He shall be your fear, and He shall be your dread. Then He shall become a sanctuary* (Isaiah 8:12-14).

Dread is a deadly feeling that something bad is going to happen. It is a form of speculation and it involves envisioning bad things lurking just around the corner. God does not want us to live in dread. The truth is that we have nothing to dread when we are walking with God. He has a great plan and purpose for our lives.

Prayer: Father God, from this day forward I will not be afraid. I love You and I've made up my mind to follow You, to not be conformed to this world, and to be transformed by the renewing of my mind. I have confidence in Your love, Father, and in the fact that You are always with me. I have confidence in our relationship, and I have confidence that You are going before me. Thank You for redeeming me and calling me by my name. By Your grace, Father, I will walk in confidence without fearing. In the name of Jesus I pray.

A LITTLE GUY WITH NO FEAR

In many ways I'm thankful for my physical stature, for I've learned several things through being small that I might not have learned if I were bigger. In the eighth grade I was the second smallest boy in my class. This did not trouble me, however, for I didn't see myself as being small.

I said something to a bigger kid in my school, and what I said really ticked him off. This guy weighed around 120 pounds—I weighed only 80—and he had it out for me from that day on. He must have had some issues. He began to put me down every time he saw me.

When I got on the school bus, he taunted me, saying, "Little Kirtie Schneider. Little Kirtie Schneider." I wanted to do something about it, but I was afraid of him. The other children would laugh, and I felt completely humiliated.

One day I finally made up my mind that I wasn't going to take this abuse any longer. The next day when he continued with his verbal taunting on the bus, I got off before him, stepped to the side next to the door, and waited for him to step off. As he was stepping off the bus, I punched him right in the face.

Do you know what happened after that? He never bothered me again. Now I don't recommend that we use that technique on others who get on our nerves. I do recommend, however, that we use this technique against Satan and his schemes. We need to make up our minds to not be afraid of Satan's lies. Rather, we should be able to look him in the eye and say, "No fear! Satan, I will not let you torment me any longer."

I recently had a dream in which I was living in this small, dilapidated house. Right next to this house was a beautiful, brand new, contemporary home which I knew was mine. I owned it, but was not living in it. Instead, it was occupied by squatters, trespassers who had no right to be there. In the dream I was afraid to live in my beautiful new home because I was afraid of these trespassers. They looked like human beings but I could tell they were demons, who would attack me if I tried to kick them out. The violent, cruel energy that was coming out of them was intense. Finally, I made up my mind, in the dream, to face them and kick them out of my house. I waited for the leader of these evil trespassers outside by the front door. When he walked out, I grabbed him, threw him on the ground, and started pounding his face. At first it seemed my blows were having no effect. But I was so focused and committed that I kept striking him, until suddenly he disintegrated. I heard a big "swish," as if all the air went out of him and he disappeared.

I think that there are several lessons for us from this dream. First, I believe the two houses in the dream represent spiritual realities. The run-down, small house represents the small, dark place Satan wants to keep us in, a place of fear and isolation. The large, beautiful, contemporary home is the place in the Spirit that Jesus has purchased for us. Jesus said, *"I came that they may life and have it abundantly"* (John 10:10). It is a place of freedom.

Sadly, in order for us to enter in and occupy this beautiful home in the Spirit that Yeshua has bought for us, we must drive out the squatters, the trespassers, just like Israel did to take possession of the Promised Land (see Num. 13 and Josh. 6). When we first begin to take authority over the evil spirit of fear, it may feel like nothing is happening, as it did in my dream. Don't be deceived; you are strong against the enemy. As you continue on the offense against him, he will eventually break. Such is the nature of our battle against fear—stay with it. Every time a thought or feeling of fear or anxiety comes into your mind, say to it "I reject you Satan, get out of my head." Jesus spoke to the demons. Matthew 8:16 tells us "He cast out the spirits with a word." Jesus was aggressive against darkness. He commanded Satan to get behind Him. In Matthew 4:10-11 we read "Jesus said to him 'Away from me Satan'... Then the devil left Him." Speak to the thoughts of fear that intrude in your mind. Say "Get out of my head! You're a liar, Satan, in Jesus' name!" Then focus on the truth about your situation given to you in God's Word. Jesus commanded Satan out, then He focused on the

Scriptures (see Matthew 4:1-11). Keep resisting and fighting, and you will enter into a new spiritual reality, a new spiritual house, in which you will enjoy a fuller experience of the abundant life that Jesus brought and bought for us.

Prayer: Father, help me to have divine courage to face the enemy and never be afraid of him. I will not listen to his lies any longer. Let Your love rise up like a fountain within me, casting all fear out from me. I bless You, Lord God, and I ask for Your help and deliverance. I ask for a divine quickening in my life. Bring strength and faith to me, Lord God. Help me overcome all fear.

RELATIONSHIP PROVOKES BLESSING

Before I began my ministry as a Messianic rabbi, I was also involved in the business world, working as a salesperson for a builder. I became the strongest salesperson in the company, and I believe this was because of my relationship with God. Because of this relationship, I was not afraid to make presentations, to speak to others about our services, and to close deals with our customers.

There was another man who worked for us during that time. He was well trained and had a lot of experience in the business, and I wondered why he wasn't doing as well as I was in making sales. It was because he was afraid of people—afraid to talk to them, make presentations, and to close deals. Therefore, he struggled throughout his time there.

Choosing not to be afraid is choosing to love God. How is this so? If we love God, we will not grieve Him by being afraid of what can happen to us. When we love God, we will fear and trust Him, over the fears of the world.

Prayer: Heavenly Father, I love You, and I never want to grieve You by giving in to fear. I believe You and all the promises of Your Word, not the lies of Satan. Strengthen me in faith and truth within my inner man by the Ruach HaKodesh, the precious Holy Spirit. Help me to walk always in Your covenant love and in victory. In the name of Yeshua Hamashiach I pray.

10

GOD'S GREATEST DESIRE

*Submit therefore to God. Resist the devil and
he will flee from you. Draw near to God, and
He will draw near to you* (James 4:7-8).

INTIMACY THROUGH LOVE

The most effective way to develop a shield against fear is to build a close personal relationship with the Lord. This is God's greatest desire for us, because when we are intimate with Him, fear has no entrance into our lives.

Mary spent time with Jesus while Martha was busy making preparations for His meal (Luke 10:38-42). When Martha asked Jesus to tell Mary to come and help, Jesus said to her, *"But only one thing is necessary, for Mary has chosen **the good part**, which shall not be taken away from her"* (Luke 10:42). As we choose the good part, beloved, we will have more power and authority to stand against fear.

Some people are afraid of God, causing them to not want to develop intimacy with Him. Though we are commanded to fear Him (through reverence and honor), we must not fear Him in a way that prevents love. He loves us with an unconditional love, and His love will not be taken away from us. He is not looking for ways to make our lives miserable or even ways to punish us. He wants us to get to know Him better.

"We love, because He first loved us" (1 John 4:19). God took the initiative and we responded to Him when we were saved. He did not choose us because of anything we did, either good or bad, but simply because it was His choice to love us. Paul wrote, *"But God demonstrates His own love toward us, in that while we were yet sinners, [Messiah] died for us"* (Rom. 5:8).

The love that God has for us is like the love a parent has for an infant child—tender, compassionate, and warm. *Rachum* is the first word He uses in describing His nature (Exod. 34:5-7), coming from the Hebrew term for "womb," communicating and revealing to us that the Lord loves us with the kind of affection that a mother has for her baby who came from her own womb. The Lord's love never changes, and He will never love us any more or any less than He does right now. His love is both constant and consistent.

Prayer: Father, Messiah Yeshua, we ask you to direct our hearts into the knowledge and revelation of Your love for us. *"May the Lord direct [our] hearts into the love of God and into the steadfastness of Christ"* (2 Thess. 3:5). *Amen.*

CULTIVATE INTIMACY

The theme of intimacy with God is woven throughout the Scriptures. Even the Tabernacle, which the Lord commanded the children of Israel to build, was for the purpose of having intimacy with Him: *"Let them construct a sanctuary for Me, that I may dwell among them"*

(Exod. 25:8). Yes, God desired to dwell among the Israelites, and He desires to dwell with us in the same way.

There are three primary ways to cultivate this intimacy with Him—through obedience, fasting, and spending time sitting still in His presence.

Through Obedience

Jesus said, *"He who has My commandments and keeps them is the one who loves Me; and he who loves Me will be loved by My Father, and I will love him and will disclose Myself to him. ...If anyone loves Me, he will keep My word; and My Father will love him, and We will come to him and make Our abode with him"* (John 14:21,23).

For many years I found this Scripture to be troubling to my soul. On the surface, it seemed to be saying that God would love me if I simply obeyed Him, and that God's love was somehow based on my performance—it would fluctuate on good and bad days. To think that God's love for me was based on obedience seemed to contradict the Scriptures that I had based my relationship with Him on.

As the years went by, however, Yeshua helped me understand what He was actually saying here: as I keep giving myself to Him, He will reveal His love to me. It's so important to understand that God's love for us never changes; but as we choose to love Him daily, He reveals His love to us more and more. We don't obey Him in order to receive His love; rather, we obey Him in order to walk in oneness with Him. As we do so, He reveals His love to us more and more.

In Deuteronomy 8 the Lord told the children of Israel that He loved them as a father loves his own son. He explained, however, that He could not bring them into the Promised Land until their hearts and character were prepared for it. John 14:21-23 teaches this same truth. God loves us, desires to reveal Himself to us, and wants to make His home with us—but He will not do so until we choose to love Him in response.

When Yeshua speaks of obedience, He isn't seeking obedience for obedience's sake, but rather obedience for the sake of love. Disobedience produces a separation in our life from God. As we come into more oneness with Yeshua, we will no longer be striving against Him. It will no longer be our way versus His way, but rather a joining together with Him. As we learn to say with conviction in our heart, "Lord, not my will but Thy will be done," we will enter into a deeper intimacy with our heavenly Father. The more intimate we are with God, the less fear we will have.

Through Fasting

Fasting is another way to grow in our intimacy with God. Its purpose is not to gain His favor, because He already loves us and will never love us more or less than He does right now. We see examples in the Scriptures of people who fasted in order to gain answers to their prayers, but this is not the primary purpose of fasting. The primary purpose is to gain intimacy with God.

Yeshua was asked why His disciples didn't fast, and He responded that they had no need to fast because the bridegroom was still with them. He went on to explain that when the bridegroom was taken away from them, they would fast, because they missed Him, were longing for Him, and wanted to feel closer to Him. (Mark 2:18-22).

Fasting makes us hungry for God. When we fast, we learn to look to God alone as our source for life. It helps us recognize our total dependency on Him, and it will give us a greater focus and clarity for our life, drawing us into deeper intimacy with God. This is not to say that fasting will always bring about some extraordinary or sensational miracle or that it will cause our life to be perfect. I've been disappointed after fasting because it seemed that very little happened as a result. But the truth was that something did happen, even if I wasn't aware of it at the time.

Several years ago, I prayed for an entire year for greater peace in my life. The Lord finally came to me in a dream in which I found myself in a dense, lush, and extremely green forest. It was surrounded with rock formations that were covered with lush ivy. The ivy-covered rocks hid the forest, making it a secret area, a secluded paradise.

As I beheld the lush beauty of this forest, the Spirit of God came over me in billows of peace. He kept filling me with His presence, love, and peace as He led me deeper and deeper into the forest. A little clearing emerged in which I saw a simple wooden picnic table, representing the fullness of God. As the Spirit of God led me toward the table I suddenly smelled pizza. The smell of pizza was not coming from the table, but it was taking my focus off the table. It was such a strong, pleasant aroma that it caused me to grow hungry, even though I hadn't felt hungry before I smelled it.

I wondered what I should do. On the one hand I wanted to follow the Spirit of God toward the picnic table so I could experience more and more of His peace, but on the other hand, I also wanted pizza. "Maybe I could have a piece of pizza," I thought to myself, "and then I could follow God's Spirit deeper into the forest." As soon as that thought came to me, the dream was over.

I was grieved it had come to an end. After having one of the most emotionally satisfying experiences with God that I'd ever had, I had chosen to trade it in for a tray of pizza. Falling on my knees after I got out of bed, I prayed, "Lord, forgive me. I can't believe I did that. I've been praying for an entire year for Your peace in my life, and I traded it for a lousy piece of pizza. Please give me another chance."

I went back to bed in the hopes that my dream would reoccur and that I would be able to go deeper into the lush forest with the Holy Spirit. That, however, never happened. When I awoke this time, I was even more grieved than I was before. "Why did this happen, Lord? Did Satan steal Your peace from me? Where did the pizza come from? Did You bring it to me, or was it Satan trying to rob me of what You wanted to give me?"

> **Prayer:** *Father, we pray that You will continue to reveal Your Son to us, and that we will not let any fear stand in the way of following Him. Jesus, You said that You have revealed the Father's name to Your children and that You will continue to reveal it. So we ask You to continue to reveal Yourself to us, giving us the strength and courage to follow after You without allowing fear to keep us from You.*

Even if it was Satan, I thought to myself, the Lord engineered the dream in order to show me something. I felt the Lord was saying to me, "If you will deny yourself the natural, then you will be drawn deeper into the supernatural, and you will experience more of My glory and peace. If you deny yourself the 'pizza,' the natural, for the sake of Me, you will be drawn deeper into My peace and into the supernatural." But fasting isn't just giving up pizza, the Lord may direct you to fast from TV, the Internet, certain types of food, certain relationships, or any number of things. As we deny ourselves and let go of the things Father directs us to fast from, He draws us closer to Himself.

Through fasting we deny ourselves the natural and open ourselves up to experience more of the supernatural in our lives. We must remember that this intimacy and oneness with Christ is not an overnight experience; it will not come in a single day, week, or even a month. Rather, it will take an entire lifetime to develop this kind of closeness with the Lord.

Even though I hadn't been very good at fasting, I now felt empowered by the Lord through my dream to complete a significant fast.

For the first twenty-one days I ate only one meal a day. Then for the next nineteen days I did not eat any food at all, only liquids. Then I felt led to extend it another three days, where I had no food or any liquids either. When the fast was over, I was extremely thin and emaciated.

In spite of my expectations, it seemed that nothing happened as a result of my forty-three-day fast. I didn't understand it at the time, but some important things had changed inside of me. God had done a transforming work in my life, even though it was different from what I was expecting.

The truth is that fasting always changes us—every time, whether we see the results or not. God uses it to transform us and to gain possession of us for Himself. We may or may not experience bliss and joy from fasting, but as we rely on God to be our only source, we will be drawn into greater intimacy with Him. Over time, our passion for intimacy with the Messiah will be realized and increased.

Through Soaking in His Presence

The Hebrew term for "to soak up" is *lees pog*. When we spend time in *lees pog*, we are simply sitting before the Lord, quietly resting in Him and soaking up His presence. At such times we put away all striving and talking, and we simply quietly wait and rest in Him.

Our culture today causes us to be very busy people. The result is greater strain and stress in everyone's life. Sometimes we even overburden ourselves in the pursuit of spiritual things. We believe that if we do more, we will become more; but the actual fact is that oftentimes less is more when it comes to spiritual things. We are human *beings*, not human *doings*. Yes, we should want to spend greater amounts of time with God, but we must realize that we are not given points based on time spent with Him.

God calls us to be people who put aside our busyness and the clamor of this world to spend time alone with Him every day. If we want to become intimate with Him, we must spend time in His presence. We are to discipline ourselves if true transformation is to occur.

King David found intimacy with the Lord simply by spending time in His presence on a consistent basis. He said, *"Surely I have composed and quieted my soul; like a weaned child rests against his mother, my soul is like a weaned child within me"* (Ps. 131:2). David took time every day to seek the Lord. He learned to rest in Him, and this caused him to become a man of great faith, character, and presence.

The Lord Himself demonstrated the importance of resting in the creation account. In the Book of Genesis, we read how God rested from His work on the Sabbath day after creating the world in six days. (Gen. 2:3). Did the Lord actually need to rest? Was He physically exhausted from His work? I don't think so, because He never becomes tired like you and I do. I believe He was showing us a pattern for our own lives to follow—work six days and rest on the seventh. Yeshua also spoke about the importance of rest and the need for a Sabbath: *"The Sabbath was made for man, and not man for the Sabbath"* (Mark 2:27).

The word *Sabbath* means "to rest," and resting is a creation principle that was designed by God Himself. He built the need to rest into the fabric of our lives. If we try to work 24/7, we will soon get burned out, leading to great ineffectiveness in our work and relationships. However, if we follow God's example by resting in Him, we will be blessed as He refreshes and restores us.

In a similar way, we need to set aside time each day to rest in the Lord's presence. "Soaking" in His presence are little daily "Sabbaths" meant to help us connect with God. God wants us to learn to receive from Him, not just do things for Him. We don't need to become better *doers*; instead, we need to become better *receivers*.

So many are running here and there, going to church services in many different places, reading spiritual books, watching Christian television, and doing things for the Lord, all of which can edify us, but when do they ever take time to sit quietly before the Lord? As we learn to soak up God's presence, we will enlarge our capacity to receive more from Him, and our ability to focus and meditate on Him will grow. He will make us more sensitive to the leading of the Holy Spirit.

If we want to communicate something important to someone, we don't do so when the other person's attention is on something else. We normally wait until we can have their undivided attention. And it is much the same with the Lord. He prefers not to communicate to us if our attention is on something else, distracted by our busyness. So He waits until our focus is upon Him.

It is my hope that you will make the commitment now to spend time with the Lord every day, if you are not already doing so. His presence will flow from us a result of this—a natural overflow of having communion with Him. Intimacy with God requires us to be set apart unto Him—focusing completely on Him. If we are to cultivate intimacy with Him, then we must do it through obedience, fasting, and spending time sitting still in His presence. These disciplines will strengthen us and help us in our battle to gain victory over fear.

Prayer: *Father, Thank You that You love me and have destined me to reign with You and have victory over fear. I'm excited and I feel Your love inside me. I will overcome because I am born again and Your Word says, "He that is born of God overcomes the world." Thank You, Father. I love You Jesus, amen.*

II

WALKING WITH GOD

So this I say, and affirm together with the Lord, that you walk no longer just as the Gentiles also walk, in the futility of their mind, being darkened in their understanding, excluded from the life of God because of the ignorance that is in them, because of the hardness of their heart...and that you be renewed in the spirit of your mind, and put on the new self, which in the likeness of God has been created in righteousness and holiness of the truth (Ephesians 4:17,23-24).

WALKING WITH GOD THROUGH PRAYER

Prayer: *Abba Father, thank You for allowing me to take a stand upon Your Word. Thank You for the power of prayer. Your Word says in Romans 16:20 that you will crush Satan under my feet. Father, I ask You right now in Jesus' name, Who is the Prince of Peace, to crush Satan under my feet. Thank You, Father. In the name of Jesus I pray, amen.*

DIALOGUE WITH GOD

God longs to have deep and intimate fellowship with us. There are so many voices crying for our attention in the world today. We need to be able to distinguish His voice from the others'. Prayer is not just a one-way monologue in which we list our needs. Instead, it should be a dialogue with God—talking and listening. There are seven important steps in learning how to dialogue with God.

1. Stilling Our Heart and Mind

We do this by becoming quiet before the Lord and trying to rid our environment of anything that might distract us. I have found that practicing the discipline of listening to soft worship music and reading Scriptures and a devotional first thing in the morning is very helpful. This takes discipline and involves sacrifice, but if you will stick with it I know that you will agree with me that it's worth it You will find if you do this you will have more peace and will be able to war against the enemy more effectively. Isaiah wrote, *"In repentance and rest you will be saved, in quietness and trust is your strength"* (Isa. 30:15). Quietness before the Lord causes us to gain strength for the warfare that we must wage in our lives. It brings confidence to our hearts. This is why the psalmist reminds us, *"Cease striving and know that I am God"* (Ps. 46:10).

You will gain a greater awareness of God's Spirit within you when you develop the spiritual discipline of being still before the Lord. The apostle Paul (Shaul) speaks of the importance of spiritual discipline. He tells us that *physical* discipline has some profit—but *spiritual* discipline is not only profitable now, but is profitable for eternity.

> *For bodily discipline is only of little profit, but godliness is profitable for all things, since it holds promise for the present life and also for the life to come* (1 Timothy 4:8 NASB).

We hear so little about spiritual discipline in our Western church culture. Instead, we often try to make things as easy and convenient as possible for our congregants. Too often, we hear only what we want to hear, and there is little demand placed upon our lives. In fact, many have turned Yeshua into a magic genie who exists to grant our requests, and have turned the message of the gospel into a plan to achieve the American dream. I say all this to point out that self-discipline is, oftentimes, not included in the messages that many of us are hearing today. The call to follow Yeshua is about the sacrifice of our own ambitions, and it involves self-discipline. Yeshua told us, *"For whoever wishes to save his life will lose it; but whoever loses his life for My sake will find it"* (Matt. 16:25 NASB). Yeshua also taught us, *"and anyone who does not take his cross and follow me is not worthy of me"* (Matt. 10:38).

Before Yeshua went to the cross to be crucified, He prayed to the Father in the Garden of Gethsemane saying, *"Father, if you are willing, take this cup from me; yet not my will, but yours be done"* (Luke 22:42).

Simply stated, beloved, if you are going to enter in through the straight and narrow way that leads to life, you must practice self-discipline in your life.

> *Enter through the narrow gate; for the gate is wide and the way is broad that leads to destruction, and there are many who enter through it. For the gate is small and the way is narrow that leads to life, and there are few who find it* (Matthew 7:13-14 NASB).

This self-discipline involves the practice of stilling yourself before God. The psalmist knew the importance of being still before God, *"Be still, and know that I am God"* (Ps. 46:10a).

What was true for the psalmist is true for all believers. As you learn to sit still before God and allow Him to minister to you, He will transform your life. He is the only One who can bring change. Even though you may feel nothing is happening as you sit before Him, trust the process. You probably won't see change in a single day, but over time, you will notice change in your life.

As you sit before the Lord, He will bring you into a greater understanding of who you are in Him. This greater revelation of self-understanding will bring a positive affirmation of your identity in Him as well as an understanding of the areas in your life where you have been deceived and need to repent.

As you spend time sitting in the Lord's presence and seeking Him, He promises that you, too, will be rewarded with transformation.

> *And without faith it is impossible to please God, because anyone who comes to him must believe that he exists and that he rewards those who earnestly seek him* (Hebrews 11:6).

I encourage you to designate a room somewhere in your home and spend at least 30 minutes every day sitting before the Lord with beautiful vertical worship music playing. As you spend time sitting before the Lord, He will use the music as an instrument of the Holy Spirit to impart Himself into your life. Start sitting before Him every day for 30 minutes. Everyone is capable of spending 30 minutes with God each day.

As time goes on, increase the time to an hour or more. It is of utter importance that you maintain this daily discipline; because once you allow an exception to come in, all your discipline will go right out the window. Even if you have to stay up late at night because you were so busy that day, take the time to sit before the Lord seeking Him.

Adopt an attitude of receiving instead of striving. Allow the Lord to impart to you the revelation that His Spirit is within you. As you take time to come out of the world and spend time in stillness before Him, He will impart His peace to you through His Spirit. Even if you can't sense God's presence and feel as though nothing is happening, don't give up. God sees you and your desire to draw close to Him, and He will reward you as you continue to patiently sit before Him. Remember, this is not a sprint but a marathon.

2. *Cleansing from Sin*

"If I regard wickedness in my heart," the psalmist said, *"the Lord will not hear"* (Ps. 66:18). Sin separates us from God and prevents us from having fellowship with Him. In 1 John we read,

> *If we say that we have fellowship with Him and yet walk in the darkness, we lie and do not practice the truth; but if we walk in the Light as He Himself is in the Light, we have fellowship with one another, and the blood of Jesus His Son cleanses us from all sin. If we say that we have no sin, we are deceiving ourselves and the truth is not in us. If we confess our sins, He is faithful and righteous to forgive us our sins and to cleanse us from all unrighteousness* (1 John 1:6-9).

In order to have dialogue with God, we have to confess our sins to Him on a regular basis. We cannot let sin reign in our hearts. Sure, we still sin at times, but we must come before Him confessing our sin in order to restore our fellowship. This pertains not just to our actions, but to our thoughts as well. When we have thoughts of hatred, accusation, judgement, or fear we need to stay in fellowship with God by lifting these thoughts up to Him and asking Him to forgive us and cleanse us.

3. *Be Genuine and Honest*

Inasmuch as we know that the truth sets us free, we must be truthful about everything with God. As we learned from Adam, who attempted to hide from God after sinning, He knows everything about us, and we must never attempt to cover anything up when we come to Him. As we expose our weaknesses to the Father, He replaces them with His strength. The truth is always our best friend, and the lies of the devil are always our worst enemy. The blood of Jesus forgives and cleanses from all sin.

When Paul asked God to remove his thorn in the flesh, a messenger of Satan sent forth to buffet him, God's response was, *"My grace is sufficient for you, for power is perfected in weakness."* Paul then says after this amazing revelation, *"Most gladly, therefore, I will rather boast about my weaknesses, so that the power of Christ may dwell in me"* (2 Cor. 12:9). God's greatest strength is revealed in our weakness. Paul went on to say, *"For when I am weak, then I am strong"* (2 Cor. 12:10). So let's not be afraid to be honest with God about our sin and weaknesses.

4. *Full Assurance of Faith*

"And without faith it is impossible to please Him, for he who comes to God must believe that He is and that He is a rewarder of those who seek Him" (Heb. 11:6). The Spirit of God moves through faith. Faith is like a channel that the river of God flows through. Oftentimes we can make a choice to believe. Let's choose faith and that God is. In doing so we open up a door for God to work in our lives.

5. *Wait on the Lord*

Dialogue with God requires patience. Patience is developed within us as we wait in His presence. I had a dream in which I found myself sitting in a dark room across from a man who I knew had been with me for a long time. He was on one side of the table, and I was on the other side. Somehow in the dream, I knew that this man was a familiar friend. I was tired of sitting across from him, and I wanted to leave the room because nothing seemed to be happening. It seemed boring! The Lord revealed to me that the man across the table in this dark room in which nothing seemed to be happening was Yeshua. The revelation the Lord was communicating to me was that if I just keep spending time sitting across from Yeshua, He will make me whole.

Sometimes He speaks by way of a still small voice within our spirit, and sometimes through His Word. The Holy Spirit will also speak directly to us and we need to be listening to discern His voice. Jesus said, "My sheep hear my voice" (see John 10:3-4). We also need to be listening for the voice of Jesus in our dreams at night and through simple pictures that the Holy Spirit will project upon the screens of our minds.

God speaks through dreams and visions. *"And it shall be in the last days,' God says, 'That I will pour forth of My Spirit on all mankind; and your sons and your daughters shall prophesy, and your young men shall see visions, and your old men shall dream dreams'"* (Acts 2:17). Isaiah talked of this when he wrote, *"Your ears will hear a word behind you, 'This is the way, walk in it,' whenever you turn to the right or to the left"* (Isa. 30:21). This is my prayer for you.

6. *Receive His Discipline*

The discipline of our Father is a great gift to us. Because He disciplines us we are being transformed into the image of Christ. Knowing that the Father is disciplining me is a great comfort to me. I'm not smart enough to get it all right, but His truth and discipline keep me moving forward and on the right path. "My son, do not regard lightly the discipline of the Lord, Nor faint when you are reproved by Him; For those whom the Lord loves He disciplines, And He scourges every son whom He receives. It is for discipline that you endure; God deals with you as with sons; for what son is there whom his father does not discipline? But if you are without discipline, of which all have become partakers, then you are illegitimate children and not sons. Furthermore, we had earthly fathers to discipline us, and we respected them; shall we not much rather be subject to the Father of spirits, and live? For they disciplined us for a short time as seemed best to them, but He disciplines us for our good, so that we may share His holiness. All discipline for the moment seems not to be joyful, but sorrowful; yet to those who have been trained by it, afterwards it yields the peaceful fruit of righteousness" (Heb 12:5-11). We are to accept this truth, remembering that the truth will make us free.

7. *Do Not Be Afraid*

As we dialogue with God, all fear must go. Let me share a story with you that illustrates this.

When one of my daughters was away in college, my wife and I went to visit her. We went out to dinner together, and I could tell something was bothering her. So I asked her, "Are you okay?"

Her response was disturbing to me. She said, "I am afraid that something bad is going to happen to you. I'm afraid you are going to die today."

This was a real fear for her, and I knew it was coming from the enemy because it was a feeling of dread and gloom. I said, "Honey, let's pray." We joined our hands together and I prayed, "Father, we take a stand against the enemy in my daughter's life. Fill her with Your love and remove this fear from her. In Jesus' name I come against Satan, and I drive all fear away from my daughter. We take authority over the spirit of fear. Father, we ask you to protect us. Thank you, for Your love and protection in Jesus's Name."

She replied emphatically, "Amen!" Yeshua broke the power of fear. This is how my wife and I always dealt with fear that attacked our daughters. Prayer is a mighty force to be reckoned with.

Romans 15:13: *"Now may the God of hope fill you with all joy and peace in believing, so that you will abound in hope by the power of the Holy Spirit."* As this becomes a reality in our lives, all fear will be extinguished and we will have true dialogue with God. Through these seven steps we can have deep and intimate dialogue with God.

PURITY OF HEART AND MIND

Having a pure heart and mind is necessary in developing intimacy with God. Let me share a dream I had that illustrates this point. My wife and I were going on a cross-country road trip. About halfway through our journey, we stopped at the home of my former martial arts instructor and asked if we could spend the night with him. He graciously agreed and said, "Sure, come in."

He took us upstairs, but instead of taking us to the bedroom where we would be spending the night, he took us into the bathroom. We all looked into the toilet bowl together. The water in the bowl was blue, because it had blue sanitizer in it.

Next, I was astonished when I saw my friend, the martial arts instructor, who was about six foot two, dive into the toilet bowl. We saw him in the blue water in the toilet bowl and he was encased in a translucent bubble, which was the shape of an egg. He was reduced in size to about seven inches. He was very joyful and happy inside the translucent bubble and surrounded by the blue sanitizer.

All of a sudden he jumped out of the bowl and stood next to me in full life size once again. Then he led us to the bedroom where my wife and I were going to spend the night. My wife and I got into bed, went to sleep, and the next morning when we woke up, we made the bed and then walked downstairs.

We were ready to continue with our journey, so we thanked the martial arts instructor for his kindness to us. "Before you go," he said, "we are going to go back upstairs and check the room where you were sleeping." We followed him up the stairs to the room we had slept in, and he pulled a dresser away from the wall. He said, "No, you're not going to go yet. We're going to see how clean this room really is." He then took a toothbrush and began to scrub the wall by the baseboard behind the dresser. I remember thinking, "What in the world is he doing? I slept here for only one night; why in the world is he scrubbing the wall with a toothbrush?" I was in a state of shock and disbelief at this point.

Then he pointed to another section of the wall that had been behind the dresser, and I noticed there was a wire coming from the baseboard area with a strange gizmo attached to it. I had never seen anything like it before. He said, "Reset it." So I got on my knees and saw a button on it, so I pressed it. He loudly said, "No! You're not doing it right! You're not thinking." He got on his knees and opened the gadget. On the inside there were several buttons, and he pressed about three of them to reset the device.

As I sought the Lord about the dream, I believe He was showing me: "You know, you're on a journey with Me. You're halfway through this journey, and you've cleaned up a lot of the outer things in your life. But before you can continue this journey with Me, I want to sanitize you in a deeper way. As I do so, it will make you joyful in Me."

I had thought that making the bed we had slept in was enough, but the Lord was showing me that He wanted more than just surface things cleaned up in my life. The electrical wire and gizmo represented my mind and thoughts. Even as the gizmo needed to be reset, so did my thoughts.

The Lord was showing me that in order to move forward with Him, my thoughts needed to be cleansed. In the dream, when the martial arts instructor, who I believe was a symbol of the Lord, said "You're not thinking," the Lord was showing me that even as I tried to reset the gizmo without thinking about what I was doing, so too, I was allowing my mind to be on auto-pilot without being intentional with my thoughts. I realized that on this journey with Him I had made significant progress, even as my martial arts instructor's home was halfway to my destination point in the dream. The Lord was revealing to me that to continue on my journey to a deeper place in Him, my thoughts needed to be cleansed.

The blue sanitization fluid in the toilet bowl represented cleansing from sin and defilement. And the martial artist in the toilet bowl was joyful because the Lord was showing me how much of His joy I will have as He cleanses me.

We have to reprogram our minds by replacing thoughts of fear with thoughts of truth, God's love, and His Word. If we do not do this consistently, we will not be able to continue our journey with the Lord. We will be stuck right where we are.

To go deeper with the Lord, let's pray, *"O Lord, you have searched me and known me. You know when I sit down and when I rise up; You understand my thought from afar. You scrutinize my path and my lying down, and are intimately acquainted with all my ways"* (Ps. 139:1-3).

Prayer: *Father, I pray right now that You would take the foul spirit of fear completely away from me. Help me to remember that fear grieves You and that Satan is laughing because he has Your children trapped in fear, and not trusting You. I repent, Father, of all the times when I've feared and grieved You. I want to be one with You, and I want to hear Your voice speaking to me. Thank You for Your loving-kindness, which is better than life to me. In Messiah's name.*

GOD IS OUR SHIELD

David said to God, *"But You, O Lord, are a shield about me, my glory, and the One who lifts my head"* (Ps. 3:3). In order for us to walk with God more intimately, we must believe that God is reigning in our circumstances, each and every day. He is paying attention to the details of our life and He is not going to leave us alone.

Jacob was sleeping with his head on a rock; in a dream he saw a ladder ascending from heaven to earth, and angels of God were ascending and descending upon it. When he woke up, he said, *"Surely the Lord is in this place, and I did not know it"* (Gen. 28:16). What place was he referring to? He was referring to the place where he was lying, that God was with him in his life, in his current circumstances. Through this experience he gained the confidence to know that he wasn't alone.

I read the testimony of a man who went to a healing crusade. He particularly noticed one child who was in a wheelchair—the child's body was twisted and he looked so uncomfortable. He hoped the child would be healed during the crusade. However, at the end of the meeting, he noticed this child was still there in the same wheelchair. The man got mad at God and wondered, "Why wasn't that child healed?"

All of a sudden, the Lord opened the man's eyes to see that the child in the wheelchair was in the bubble of God's presence. It looked terrible from the outside, but God saw the situation entirely differently. The child was immersed in God's love and mercy, and was at peace in the *shalom* of the Lord.

Instead of being deceived by what our eyes see, we need to see with the eyes of God's Spirit. The child was more at peace than the man who was worried about him. We must make up our mind to trust God, regardless of what is taking place around us. God is with us and He is our shield.

THE BATTLE: OUR IMAGINATION

"What will happen tomorrow? Will I run out of money? Will I get sick?" These kinds of thoughts stir up images in our imagination as we press on to walk with God. He does not want us to use our imagination to envision and project all kinds of disasters that *could* happen someday. To do so is to use our imagination for evil. In fact, it is actually sinful to do so.

When my children were young, I used to worry about them every night before I went to bed. "Will they be okay tomorrow? Will something bad happen to them tonight?" I constantly worried as I tucked them in. I know many parents share similar fears about their children. They might wonder, "Will my children get in trouble at school? Will they get in with the wrong crowd? Will they start using drugs? Will they be safe? Will they get into an accident? Will they get sick? Will somebody attack or violate them?"

But instead of thinking such negative thoughts, we must take an offensive and proactive position and use our imagination to envision the good things of God. God designed our imagination to meditate upon Him and His Word, not on the bad things that could happen in the future. "'For I know the plans that I have for you,' declares the Lord, 'plans for welfare and not for calamity to give you a future and a hope'" (Jer 29:11).

David wrote, *"Surely goodness and lovingkindness will follow me all the days of my life, and I will dwell in the house of the Lord forever"* (Ps. 23:6). And Paul says we are to cast down every thought that presents itself against the knowledge of God:

> *For though we walk in the flesh, we do not war according to the flesh, for the weapons of our warfare are not of the flesh, but divinely powerful for the destruction of fortresses. We are destroying speculations and every lofty thing raised up against the knowledge of God, and we are taking every thought captive to the obedience of Christ* (2 Corinthians 10:3-5).

A battle is taking place within our mind and imagination. The way to win this battle is to destroy all speculations (including worries and fears) and every lofty thing that opposes the knowledge of God. We are to take captive all thoughts to the obedience of Christ. Each day is a battle. And each day we must decide what thoughts we will choose and focus on.

Prayer: *Help me, Father, to stop worrying about tomorrow. I come against every foul thought and mental stronghold that causes me to fear. I trade in all worries and receive Your peace in place of them. Help me to use the weapons of the warfare that You've given to me to defeat fear. In the name of Messiah Jesus, help me to destroy the enemy's fortresses and everything that opposes You. I bring all my thoughts and my imagination captive to the obedience of Christ.*

WALK IN A MANNER WORTHY OF GOD

As believers, we are told to *"walk in a manner worthy of the Lord, to please Him in all respects, bearing fruit in every good work and increasing in the knowledge of God"* (Col. 1:10). Therefore, we must walk:

- in newness of life (Rom. 6:4),

- honestly, as in the day (Rom. 13:13),

- by faith, not by sight (2 Cor. 5:7),

- in the Spirit, so we will not fulfill the lusts of the flesh (Gal. 5:16),

- worthy of the vocation to which we have been called (Col. 1:10),

- in wisdom (Col. 4:5),

- in the light (1 John 1:7),

- after His commandments (2 John 6), and

- in truth (3 John 4).

As we learn to walk in the ways I've outlined above, fear will no longer have a stronghold over us. We will be guided one step at a time, one day at a time, and one moment at a time by the Lord. He holds our hands every step of the way.

Prayer: *Yeshua, I thank You that You are walking beside me each step of the way. Because this is true, I do not need to fear anything or anyone. Help me to walk in a way that will please You. Help me to seek first Your kingdom and Your righteousness. Help me to keep on keeping on and to never give up, even when the warfare is most intense. You are my light and my salvation. In Your name I pray.*

12

THE POWER OF THE HOLY SPIRIT

Or do you not know that your body is a temple of the Holy Spirit who is in you, whom you have from God, and that you are not your own? (1 Corinthians 6:19)

THE RUACH HAKODESH

Before Jesus ascended back to the Father, He promised us, *"But you shall receive power when the Holy Spirit has come upon you; and you shall be My witnesses both in Jerusalem, and in all Judea and Samaria, and even to the remotest part of the earth"* (Acts 1:8). His power is at work within us, causing our minds to be renewed and our hearts to be changed as we are being formed into the image of Christ.

Some time ago I was trapped in a common deception of blaming others for my mistakes, shortcomings, and frustrations. "It's your fault!" was my response to many frustrating situations instead of accepting the blame. This kind of blame shifting is a sure sign that the Holy Spirit needs to work within our hearts, and reveals that we have a long way to go in maturing in godliness.

At that time I was a very angry person. My wife, Cynthia, and I have two very distinct personality types. She is an easygoing, relational type of person, but I tend to be very intense and driven. Sometimes the contrast between us would become a challenge for me (as I'm sure it was for her), especially when it came to keeping appointments. I always like to be on time for appointments, whereas Cynthia is more laid back about it. This often became a source of frustration for me. I tried asking, begging, pleading, and screaming at her, but nothing seemed to work.

We had been married for fifteen years, but this was still a source of friction between us. We had an important appointment coming up in a few days, so I kept reminding Cynthia of the time of the appointment: "Now, remember, we must be there at six o'clock," in the hopes that she would be on time.

When the particular evening came, I went out to wait for my wife in the car. I told her, in the nicest tone I could, that I would be waiting for her outside in the car. I waited and waited and waited. Fifteen minutes later, I became so enraged that I almost put the gas pedal to the floor to ram my vehicle right through the garage door!

It was then that I realized something was wrong with me. I discovered that my rage was out of control and that I had a problem. After all, whom would I have hurt by ramming my car through my garage door? I recognized that my behavior was coming from fear—a fear that others would think negatively of me for being late.

This wasn't just Cynthia's problem; it was mine. I began to own the problem for the first time in my life. I sought the Lord for a deeper understanding of my problem, and He showed me that I had been blaming my wife for my own anger. The problem wasn't only that my wife struggled with being late; rather, the problem was my anger, and my not taking responsibility for it. I was not controlling my response to her or to the situation.

While waiting on the Lord about this issue, I learned many things. The Holy Spirit began to show me so much that needed to be fixed in my life. Jesus said, *"I will ask the Father, and He will give you another Helper, that He may be with you forever; that is the Spirit of truth, whom the world cannot receive, because it does not see Him or know Him, but you know Him because He abides with you and will be in you"* (John 14:16-17). I thank God that the *Ruach HaKodesh* (Holy Spirit) lives within me. The Holy Spirit convicted me, then empowered and taught me how to overcome my anger. He continues to teach me and show me what I need to know.

OVERCOMING POWER

By the power of the Holy Spirit we can overcome the enemy's attacks. We read seven times in the chapters 2 and 3 of Revelation that we will receive an inheritance when we overcome.

- *"To him who overcomes, I will grant to eat of the tree of life which is in the Paradise of God"* (Rev. 2:7).

- *"He who overcomes will not be hurt by the second death"* (Rev. 2:11).

- *"To him who overcomes, to him I will give some of the hidden manna, and I will give him a white stone, and a new name written on the stone which no one knows but he who receives it"* (Rev. 2:17).

- *"He who overcomes, and he who keeps My deeds until the end, to him I will give authority over the nations"* (Rev. 2:26).

- *"He who overcomes will thus be clothed in white garments; and I will not erase his name from the book of life, and I will confess his name before My Father, and before His angels"* (Rev. 3:5).

- *"He who overcomes, I will make him a pillar in the temple of My God, and he will not go out from it anymore; and I will write on him the name of My God, and the name of the city of My God, the new Jerusalem, which comes down out of heaven from My God, and My new name"* (Rev. 3:12).

- *"He who overcomes, I will grant to him to sit down with Me on my throne, as I also overcame and sat down with My Father on His throne"* (Rev. 3:21).

God promises us so much when we overcome in Christ. In Him we are called to overcome the world and all that is in it; at the top of this list, is fear.

NEVER GIVE UP

We are engaged in a heavy warfare, beloved, and sometimes we are tempted to give up. Even if we fail, we must get up again, brush ourselves off, and realize that the Holy Spirit will always be with us. His power will be perfected in our weakness and we will overcome as we keep clinging to and depending on Him. The Lord says that it is *"not by might nor by power, but My Spirit"* (Zech. 4:6). The Holy Spirit will continue to impart His strength to us. We are being transformed from strength to strength, and from glory to glory, and as God's children we will overcome.

Prayer: Father, I trust You with my heart. I know You are with me. Thank You for Your help. Through You I will be more than a conqueror, a true overcomer in the face of the enemy. This causes my heart to rejoice. You are able to do far more abundantly beyond all that I could ever ask or think, according to the power that works within me. To You be the glory. Amen.

EVEN IN THE HARD TIMES

At one point, I was working as a graveyard dishwasher in California. I was 24 years old, and riding a bicycle to work because I had no car. Although this was a hard time in my life, God was doing a great work in me by making me dependent on Him and His Spirit. "For momentary, light affliction is producing for us an eternal weight of glory far beyond all comparison, while we look not at the things which are seen, but at the things which are not seen; for the things which are seen are temporal, but the things which are not seen are eternal" (2 Cor 4:17-18).

Thank God for the hard times in life as well as the pleasant times. As we cling to Him through the hard times, His Spirit will make us strong and empower us to defeat fear.

Prayer: Dear Lord God, strengthen me with divine energy, divine power, divine life, and with the fire of the Holy Spirit. Strengthen me so that I would truly take hold of Your Word and believe it with all my heart. Let it soak into the depths of my being. Help me to apply Your Word to my daily life, to stay in Your Word, and to abide in it at all times. May I never stumble as a result of seeing the things of this world. Help me to be strong and courageous, like Joshua was. He truly was a mighty man of valor, and I want to be that kind of person as well. Through Yeshua, my Messiah, I pray. Amen.

13

THE MARVELOUS GRACE OF OUR LOVING LORD

But by the grace of God I am what I am, and His
grace toward me did not prove vain; but I labored
even more than all of them, yet not I, but the grace
of God was with me (1 Corinthians 15:10).

GOD'S ALL-SUFFICIENT GRACE

Most of Paul's letters begin the same way: *"Grace to you and peace from God our Father and the Lord Jesus Christ"* (1 Cor. 1:3, 2 Cor. 1:2, Gal. 1:3, Eph 1:2, Phil. 1:2, 2 Thess. 1:2, Philem. 1:3). His grace is His favor that is poured out upon His children even when we do not deserve it. Are you afraid of suffering? God's grace is sufficient for you. Are you afraid of growing old? God's grace is sufficient for you. Are you afraid of dying? God's grace is sufficient for you, beloved. No matter what your fear might be, God's grace is there for you, empowering you to be free from fear, to overcome and be victorious.

Because God's grace is at work in our lives, there is nothing to fear. He will be with us and His grace will be working on our behalf. Jesus has overcome the world on our behalf. Through Him we can overcome the world as well.

Look at how God's grace helped the apostle Paul in the midst of hardship. He said:

> And now, behold, bound by the Spirit, I am on my way to Jerusalem, not knowing what will happen to me there, except that the Holy Spirit solemnly testifies to me in every city, saying that bonds and afflictions await me. But I do not consider my life of any account as dear to myself, so that I may finish my course and the ministry which I received from the Lord Jesus, to testify solemnly of the gospel of the grace of God (Acts 20:22-24).

Knowing that suffering awaited him, many tried to dissuade him from going, but Paul answered, *"What are you doing by weeping and breaking my heart? Don't you know that I am ready not only to be bound but to die for the sake of the gospel?"* (Acts 21:13-14). Paul had no fear of suffering because God's amazing grace had set him free from fear. He was ready to die for the sake of Messiah Jesus. It's possible for us to have this same strength from the Holy Spirit, empowering us to go through any situation we may face without fear.

Prayer: God, I come to You now in the name of Yeshua, seeking Your grace and strength to help me. Thank You, Father, for Your all-sufficient grace that will see me through. Thank You for strengthening me to face all the circumstances of my life. Strengthen me, Yeshua, to face life and all its circumstances without fear by Your Spirit, Your truth, and Your Word.

GRACE FOR SOCIAL FEARS

God's grace will take us through everything, including social fears.

Some people go through life with a terrible fear of other people, which at its root is often a fear of rejection. It may cause us to be afraid of witnessing. When we are afraid of people for fear of rejection or ridicule we grieve the Holy Spirit, who desires us to let our light shine, and be witnesses for Jesus.

Jesus desires us to be a light upon a hill; so we cannot hide our light from others. Everyone in this world of darkness needs to see the light of Christ emanating from us. Jesus said,

> *You are the salt of the earth; but if the salt has become taste-less, how can it be made salty again? It is no longer good for anything, except to be thrown out and trampled under foot by men. You are the light of the world. A city set on a hill cannot be hidden; nor does anyone light a lamp and put it under a basket, but on the lampstand, and it gives light to all who are in the house. Let your light shine before men in such a way that they may see your good works, and glorify your Father who is in heaven* (Matthew 5:13-16).

Some will see our good works, but unless we tell them about Jesus, how will they know to glorify our Father in heaven? They may think we're wonderful people, but this will not bring glory to God. They may even want to be like us, but unless we also tell them about Jesus how will our lives bring glory to God?

The presence of Christ should exude from our life in both word and deed, and then they will understand where our goodness comes from. People need to hear the word of Messiah Jesus proclaimed in order to have faith in Him. Paul reminds us that *"For whoever will call upon the name of the Lord will be saved. How then will they call on Him in whom they have not believed? How will they believe in Him whom they have not heard? And how will they hear without a preacher?" "faith comes from hearing, and hearing by the word of Christ"* (Rom. 10:13-14, 17).

To worry about what someone thinks of us, especially when sharing our faith, is an evil fear that puts the focus on us rather than on God. Jesus said, *"For what does it profit a man to gain the whole world, and forfeit his soul? For what will a man give in exchange for his soul? For whoever is ashamed of Me and My words in this adulterous and sinful generation, the Son of Man will also be ashamed of him when he comes in the glory of His Father with the holy angels"* (Mark 8:36-38).

We don't have a choice about this; we must overcome all fears, including our social fears and fear of rejection. We must choose to be more concerned about obeying Jesus than with what people think of us. We need to rise above the fear of man. We can be an effective witness because the Holy Spirit empowers us to do so. As we step out in faith, God's grace will enable us to do what we thought we could not do. In all likelihood we will be rejected by some. But praise God, Yeshua said, *"Blessed are those who have been persecuted for the sake of righteousness, for theirs is the kingdom of heaven. Blessed are you when people insult you and persecute you, and falsely say all kinds of evil against you because of Me. Rejoice and be glad, for your reward in heaven is great; for in the same way they persecuted the prophets who were before you"* (Matt. 5:10-12).

GRACE FOR PERSECUTION

Even though I have suffered persecution from my family and the Jewish community, I thank God for it. I experienced His joy while being persecuted. I took comfort in the words of Jesus, and He truly was my only friend at the time—and what a friend He is.

Yeshua's words brought great comfort to my heart:

> *If the world hates you, you know that it has hated Me before it hated you. If you were of the world, the world would love its own; but because you are not of the world, but I chose you out of the world, because of this the world hates you.... If they persecuted Me, they will also persecute you.... But all*

these things they will do to you for My name's sake, because they do not know the One who sent Me (John 15:18-21).

Throughout the years I have been the victim of rejection and even hostility, but praise God my faith in Yeshua has remained strong. If we are rejected and suffer for Him, we should consider it a privilege. *"If we endure, we will also reign with Him"* (2 Tim. 2:12). The best way to remove the fear of witnessing from our life is to simply be obedient and do it.

> *More than that, I count all things to be loss in view of the surpassing value of knowing Christ Jesus my Lord, for whom I have suffered the loss of all things, and count them but rubbish so that I may gain Christ, and may be found in Him, not having a righteousness of my own derived from the Law, but that which is through faith in Christ, the righteousness which comes from God on the basis of faith, that I may know Him and the power of His resurrection and the fellowship of His sufferings, being conformed to His death; in order that I may attain to the resurrection from the dead. Not that I have already obtained it or have already become perfect, but I press on so that I may lay hold of that for which also I was laid hold of by Christ Jesus* (Philippians 3:8-12).

THE LORD IS OUR HELPER

Let us boldly proclaim, *"The Lord is my helper, I will not be afraid. What will man do to me?"* (Heb. 13:6). He will enable us to do what we need to do, to say what we need to say, and to be what we need to be. (That's what grace is all about.) *"When they bring you before the synagogues and the rulers and the authorities, do not worry about how or what you are to speak in your defense, or what you are to say; for the Holy Spirit will teach you in that very hour what you ought to say"* (Luke 12:11-12).

If people oppose us, we should see them as instruments in God's hands to refine us. Sometimes our trials can be stepping stones to great spiritual progress.

Joseph's brothers actually hated him to the point of plotting to kill him. When Joseph came to check on them as a favor to his father, they threw him into an empty pit and then sold him into slavery to some Midianite traders who took him to Egypt. The biography of Joseph is a powerful story of a suffering servant who held on to his faith all the way through his life, and how God promoted and rewarded him for his faithfulness (Gen. 37–50).

Eventually, his brothers came back to him and said, *"Behold, we are your servants"* (Gen. 50:18). Joseph's response was quite forgiving: *"Do not be afraid, for am I in God's place? As for you, you meant evil against me, but God meant it for good"* (Gen. 50:19-20).

Sometimes God allows us to go through difficult times, in order to advance us. Whatever we are going through, God can bring good out of it, and we will be stronger as a result of it. God does not waste our pain or our hard circumstances. He redeems them for His glory.

The Lord is our helper. As we side with God in the battle, we will win in life. We will be able to shout with Paul, *"But thanks be to God, who gives us the victory through our Lord Jesus Christ"* (1 Cor. 15:57). God's grace will take over our lives as we yield to and obey Him. *"Surely goodness and lovingkindness will follow me all the days of my life, And I will dwell in the house of the Lord forever"* (Ps 23:6).

There is not one fear that is more powerful than the death and resurrection of Jesus Christ, which has the power to deliver us from all fear.

Prayer: *Father God, I ask You now for the grace I need to be a faithful witness for You even when I am persecuted for Your sake. It is a privilege for me to suffer and be rejected because of my faith in You. Yeshua, you said I am blessed when I am persecuted for righteousness sake. (See Matt 5:11-12). I have made up my mind to obey You. Because I know it grieves You when I have fear, I choose to reject fear in Jesus's name. I desire to magnify You, Father, by my words and deeds, not to magnify fear and the devil. I love You, Yeshua. Help me to show my love for You by not cowering to the fear of man. I will be a witness for You.*

14

THE VICTORIOUS LIFE

But thanks be to God, who gives us the victory through
our Lord Jesus Christ (1 Corinthians 15:57).

GOD WILL CARRY US

As I've already mentioned, when I became a believer in *Yeshua Hamashiach* our home was filled with turmoil. My parents could not understand what had happened to their Jewish son. They were greatly distressed, upset, and angry about this. They took it as a personal insult to them. How could their son, who had been *bar mitzvahed* in a Jewish synagogue, receive Jesus? To them, it was just like a slap in the face.

Of course, none of this was my intention. I did not want to offend anyone, but Jesus had revealed Himself to me in such a miraculous way that I became alive for Him! They felt like their only choice was to throw me out of the house. I can now understand where they were coming from, and in some ways I feel bad for them. They didn't receive or understand the revelation I had received. To them I was nuts.

I'll never forget the first day on my own, after being thrown out of the house. It felt as if the whole world was bathed in peace. I can't really explain this phenomenon, but it was as if I was surrounded by God's *shalom*. The peace I experienced was tangible. It was God supernaturally intervening in my life, bearing me up, and carrying me through this traumatic event. It was a gift of God's grace—His special favor in my life.

God will carry us and bear us up through every circumstance we face. Things may look terrible to someone that is only looking at the situation from the outside, but the mystery is that God surrounds His own with His invisible peace.

It is for this reason that we don't need to fear any situation. When we have thoughts of dread about the future, it is because we are envisioning a scenario where God is not present. But God will be present, and for this reason, we do not have to be afraid. I remember a woman in our congregation who was terrified of losing her job. She had been worrying about it, dreading it, for months. Then one day her boss called her into his office and fired her. She said that when it happened she had complete peace. Why? Because God was with her when it happened. It will never be as bad as what we imagine because in our fearful imaginations we are not perceiving His presence with us. But in reality, when we face any difficulty, His presence is with us, and for that reason it is not nearly as bad as we've imagined. It's kind of like this, when you look out over the ocean from the shore, you see big waves rolling in, but by the time they get to the shore, they are little ripples. The things we fear are like big waves. But when we face them, they are actually little ripples because God is with us.

MAGNIFY THE LORD WITH ME

How could Daniel go into the lions' den and not be afraid? How could he stand in the midst of hungry lions and not experience fear? It's because he was experiencing God's presence through a supernatural grace and peace that was given to Him in his situation. God does the same thing today for you and me. An extra measure of grace is given to us when we are in difficult circumstances. Beloved, having confidence in God's presence with us sets us free.

Daniel magnified God in his heart; he made God bigger and more important than the lions. Now, of course we can't make God bigger than He already is because He is omnipresent, meaning He is everywhere. But we can make Him bigger in our hearts and minds when we honor Him and worship Him. It's not that He grows, but rather our sight and awareness of Him increases. This is why David wrote, *"O magnify the Lord with me, and let us exalt His name together"* (Ps. 34:3). God is bigger than our fears.

It was through this magnification of the Lord that Shadrach, Meshach, and Abednego were able to go into the fiery furnace without fear. Can you imagine that? I think most people would say that being burned to death is the most horrifying way to die. But these men said, "Our God is able to deliver us, but even if He does not do so, we will not bow down, O king" (see Dan. 3:17-18). They saw God as being far bigger than their problem, and that's why they were victorious. In order for us to be like them, we must magnify God in our heart.

As we learn to magnify the Lord, we will be encouraged and strengthened. Courage will build within us. As the people were speaking of stoning David, he was greatly distressed, but he did not give in to fear; instead, he encouraged himself in the Lord and refused to give in to any mental imagery that included suffering and death. *"Moreover David was greatly distressed because the people spoke of stoning him, for all the people were embittered, each one because of his sons and daughters. But David strengthened himself in the Lord his God"* (1 Sam. 30:6). I love David's spirit of determination. He wasn't going to let anything, including a possible stoning, get in the way of loving God.

WE ARE BLESSED

In these difficult economic times, we need to trust in Father and Yeshua to protect us and sustain us. Do you remember what David said, *"I've never seen the righteous forsaken or his descendents begging bread"* (Ps. 37:25)? We can overcome all fears, including financial fears. We must believe we are blessed and that God's blessing will remain upon us through everything. *"Though the mountains be shaken and the hills be removed, yet my unfailing love for you will not be shaken nor my covenant of peace be removed,' says the Lord, who has compassion on you."* (Isaiah 54:10)

In the Book of Deuteronomy we read these exciting words:

> *All these blessings will come upon you and overtake you if you obey the Lord your God: Blessed shall you be in the city, and blessed shall you be in the country. Blessed shall be the offspring of your body and the produce of your ground and the offspring of your beasts, the increase of your herd and the young of your flock. Blessed shall be your basket and your kneading bowl. Blessed shall you be when you come in, and blessed shall you be when you go out. The Lord shall cause your enemies who rise up against you to be defeated before you; they will come out against you one way and will flee before you seven ways. The Lord will command the blessing upon you in your barns and in all that you put your hand to, and He will bless you in the land which the Lord your God gives you. The Lord will establish you as a holy people to Himself.... The Lord will make you the head and not the tail, and you only will be above, and you will not be underneath, if you listen to the commandments of the Lord your God, which I charge you today, to observe them carefully, and do not turn aside from any of the words which I command you today, to the*

right or to the left, to go after other gods to serve them (Deuteronomy 28:2-9, 13-14).

As we seek God and put Him first in our lives we will be blessed.

*"Blessed is the man who trusts in the Lord and whose trust is the Lord. For he will be like a tree planted by the water, that extends its roots by a stream and **will not fear when the heat comes**; But its leaves will be green, **and it will not be anxious** in a year of drought nor cease to yield fruit"* (Jer. 17:7-8).

> ***Prayer:*** *Father, help me to learn how to encourage myself in You. Thank You for bearing me up and helping me through the various circumstances of my life. I ask for an extra measure of your supernatural grace to go through difficult times victoriously like Daniel did in the lions' den. I want to magnify You at all times, and I am determined not to let anything get in the way of loving You. I praise Your holy name, and I love You, Father! Amen.*

THE MOTHER OF ALL FEARS

The fear of death may well be the root cause of all fear. Death represents the ultimate loss of control in a person's life. It is impossible for us to know what dying will be like or when we will pass away. Therefore, death is an unknown entity for all of us. Death seems so final to us, but, as many of us know, it is not final at all.

People of all ages, including children, fear death. In the Book of Hebrews we read these important words: *"Therefore, since the children share in flesh and blood, He Himself likewise also partook of the same, that through death He might render powerless him who had the power of death, that is, the devil, and might free those who through fear of death were subject to slavery all their lives"* (Heb. 2:14-15). The fear of death enslaves us unless we learn to overcome it through faith in the Word of God.

I remember being terrified of death even as a young child. My fear of being poisoned and ultimately dying was an irrational fear. I thank God that He delivered me from it when I developed a relationship with Messiah Jesus. For many people the fear of death is so intense that they can't sleep at night. You may fear death without even being aware of it. It may manifest itself instead in the form of other fears and phobias.

Because the fear of death is the fear of the unknown, of being out of control, we must go to the One who knows everything and is in control of all. God told Abram to leave the land of his fathers and to go to a land that He would show him. Abram obeyed even though his destination was unknown and he had plenty of reason to fear. In effect, God said, *"Leave your comfort zone, Abram. I am going to take you to a land of milk and honey, and I'm going to bless you and your offspring"* (Gen. 12:1-3).

Was there a risk involved? Yes, but it was the risk of faith. And really there isn't a whole lot of risk involved when we are proceeding in faith. The writer of Hebrews says that it was *"by faith Abraham, when he was called, obeyed by going out to a place which he was to receive for an inheritance; and he went out, not knowing where he was going"* (Heb. 11:8). This is true even with regard to dying. We must have faith! Many of us struggle with being certain that we will go to heaven. The Bible says, *"These things I have written to you who believe in the name of the Son of God, so that you may know that you have eternal life"* (1 John 5:13).

Most people are afraid of change, and certainly death is a major change that each of us must face. We face it by trusting God to take us into the unknown.

The Bible says that *"there is an appointed time for everything.... A time to give birth and a time to die"* (Eccles. 3:1-2). But there is nothing to fear, for Jesus said,

> *Do not let your heart be troubled; believe in God, believe also in Me. In My Father's house are many dwelling places; if it were not so, I would have told you; for I go to prepare a place for you. If I go and prepare a place for you, I will come again and receive you to Myself, that where I am, there you may be also, and you know the way where I am going* (John 14:1-4).

Prayer: *Fortify me with Your peace, O God, by Your grace. Help me to fully grasp that I will live forever with You in heaven. There is no reason for me to fear death or anything else, for that matter, for I am Yours and You are mine. Thank You!*

The great news is that when we die, we will be with Jesus, enjoying the dwelling place He is preparing for us right now. That is why the word "gospel" means "good news."

> *"Jesus said to her, 'I am the resurrection and the life; he who believes in Me will live even if he dies, and everyone who lives and believes in Me will never die'"* (John 11:25-26).

Prayer: *Father, I am looking forward to spending all eternity with You. Help me to overcome the fear of death through the power of Your Word. Yeshua, thank You for preparing a place for me where I will be able to dwell with You after I die. I bless You for delivering me from the fear of death, the fear of dying, the fear of hell, the fear of suffering, the fear of the unknown, and the fear of losing control. Through You I conquer and take authority over Satan right now, and I put his lies and fear under Your feet. I magnify You, Lord God. Thank You for the gift of heaven through Messiah Jesus.*

WE ARE VICTORS

For here we do not have a lasting city, but we are seeking the city which is to come" (Heb. 13:14). One day everything in this world will be left behind. Keeping this in mind, let us prepare for the next life by living this life victoriously and obediently.

God has made every provision for us to live in victory over fear. Victory is achievable. The fact is that Messiah Jesus has already achieved it for us. It's done. He has risen from the dead, conquered Satan, and conquered fear. Our response to this truth must be to believe it, receive it, and act upon it.

Choose not to believe the devil's lies any longer. In the same way that Messiah came to me and called me out of this world of darkness, He is calling me to walk in victory each and every day. There are still battles to fight, but I know He is enabling us to be effective in warfare, able to face all assaults *"as a good soldier of Jesus Christ"* (2 Tim. 2:3) and be victorious.

Who will separate us from the love of Christ? Will tribulation, or distress, or persecution, or famine, or nakedness, or peril, or sword? But in all these things we overwhelmingly conquer through Him who loved us. For I am convinced that neither death, nor life, nor angels, nor principalities, nor things present, nor any other created thing, will be able to separate us from the love of God, which is in Christ Jesus our Lord (Romans 8:35, 37-39).

Be strong. Be courageous.

True elimination of fear will come when through the grace of God we absolutely surrender and entrust our lives to King Jesus. When we are willing to let go of everything and abandon ourselves completely to Him, we will be free.

If you continue in My word, then you are truly disciples of Mine; and you will know the truth, and the truth will make you free. So if the Son makes you free, you will be free indeed (John 8:31-32,36).

Prayer: *Father God, I thank You so much that You have given me everything I need to live victoriously in this life. Help me to face fear with courage and to realize that there are no limits with You. Through the grace of Messiah, I can live my life fearlessly. Thank You, Messiah Jesus, for the victory that I have in You. Help me to look fear in the face, to be determined to conquer it, and to walk with complete confidence in You. In the name of Yeshua I pray, amen.*

15

SO, DO YOU REALLY WANT TO BE FREE?

Obviously, you struggle with fear, or you wouldn't have bought this book. Now, here is your opportunity to take action and be cleansed from fear. In Mark 4:35-41, Jesus revealed that people are afraid because they lack faith. Jesus said to His disciples… "Why are you so timid? How it is that you have no faith?" The answer to your fears is faith. So if we want to overcome fear, we need faith in God. This faith in God comes to us supernaturally by His Word. "Faith comes by hearing, and hearing by the Word of God"(Rom 10:17). So if you and I are serious about breaking off all shackles of fear, we are going to have to build up our faith through God's Word.

I am now going to give you God's divine strategy for you to be free. I have compiled powerful Scriptures that will build your faith and trust in God, empowering you to stand against fear. It's up to you! If you will spend the first 15 minutes of your day sitting quietly before the Lord, and read these Scriptures for a period of 8 weeks, I know you will be blessed. When you get to the end of the verses, go back to the beginning—15 minutes a day, every day, for 8 weeks, with no exceptions. In a short 8 week time-frame, you will marvel at what Jesus has done for you if you will follow through with this plan. The Bible teaches that spiritual discipline is necessary to advance in the Kingdom…" discipline yourself for the purpose of godliness" (see 1 Tim 4:7). Of course, to maintain your freedom, it will be necessary to repeat this discipline at regular intervals throughout your life.

"Go forth from your country, And from your relatives And from your father's house, To the land which I will show you; And I will make you a great nation, And I will bless you, And make your name great; And so you shall be a blessing; And I will bless those who bless you, And the one who curses you I will curse. And in you all the families of the earth will be blessed." —Gen. 12:1-3

Then Jacob awoke from his sleep and said, "Surely the Lord is in this place, and I did not know it." —Gen. 28:16

But Moses said to the people, "Do not fear! Stand by and see the salvation of the Lord which He will accomplish for you today; for the Egyptians whom you have seen today, you will never see them again forever. —Exodus 14:13

And they spoke to all the congregation of the sons of Israel, saying, "The land which we passed through to spy out is an exceedingly good land. If the Lord is pleased with us, then He will bring us into this land and give it to us - a land which flows with milk and honey. Only do not rebel against the Lord; and do not fear the people of the land, for they will be our prey. Their protection has been removed from them, and the Lord is with us; do not fear them." —Numbers 14:7-9

But from there you will seek the Lord your God, and you will find Him if you search for Him with all your heart and all your soul. For the Lord your God is a compassionate God; He will not fail you nor destroy you nor forget the covenant with your fathers which He swore to them. —Deut. 4:29, 31

All these blessings will come upon you and overtake you if you obey the Lord your God: "Blessed shall you be in the city, and blessed shall you be in the country. "Blessed shall be the offspring of your body and the produce of your ground and the offspring of your beasts, the increase of your herd and the young of your flock. "Blessed shall be your basket and your kneading bowl. "Blessed shall you be when you come in, and blessed shall you be when you go out. "The Lord shall cause your enemies who rise up against you to be defeated before you; they will come out against you one way and will flee before you seven ways. The Lord will command the blessing upon you in your barns and in all that you put your hand to, and He will bless you in the land which the Lord your God gives you. The Lord will establish you as a holy people to Himself, as He swore to you, if you keep the commandments of the Lord your God and walk in His ways. The Lord will make you the head and not the tail, and you only will be above, and you will not be underneath, if you listen to the commandments of the Lord your God, which I charge you today, to observe them carefully, and do not turn aside from any of the words which I command you today, to the right or to the left, to go after other gods to serve them. —Deut. 28:2-9, 13-14

Be strong and courageous, do not be afraid or tremble at them, for the Lord your God is the one who goes with you. He will not fail you or forsake you." —Deut. 31:6

Have I not commanded you? Be strong and courageous! Do not tremble or be dismayed, for the Lord your God is with you wherever you go." —Joshua 1:9

You need not fight in this battle; station yourselves, stand and see the salvation of the Lord on your behalf, O Judah and Jerusalem.' Do not fear or be dismayed; tomorrow go out to face them, for the Lord is with you." —2 Chron. 20:17

But You, O Lord, are a shield about me, My glory, and the One who lifts my head. —Psalm 3:3

You will make known to me the path of life; In Your presence is fullness of joy; In Your right hand there are pleasures forever. —Psalm 16:11

Even though I walk through the valley of the shadow of death, I fear no evil, for You are with me; Your rod and Your staff, they comfort me. 6 Surely goodness and loving kindness will follow me all the days of my life, and I will dwell in the house of the Lord forever. —Psalm 23:4, 6

The Lord is my light and my salvation; Whom shall I fear? The Lord is the defense of my life; whom shall I dread? When evildoers came upon me to devour my flesh, My adversaries and my enemies, they stumbled and fell. Though a host encamp against me, my heart will not fear; Though war arise against me, In spite of this I shall be confident.
—Psalm 27:1-3

O Magnify the Lord with me, and let us exalt His name together.
—Psalm 34:3

I have been young and now I am old, yet I have not seen the righteous forsaken or his descendants begging bread. —Psalm 37:25

As the deer pants for the water brooks, So my soul pants for You, O God. My soul thirsts for God, for the living God; When shall I come and appear before God? My tears have been my food day and night, While they say to me all day long, "Where is your God?" —Psalm 42:1-3

"Cease striving and know that I am God; I will be exalted among the nations, I will be exalted in the earth." —Psalm 46:10

When I am afraid, I will put my trust in You. In God, whose word I praise, In God I have put my trust; I shall not be afraid. What can mere man do to me? —Psalm 56:3-4

Blessed be the Lord, who daily bears our burden, The God who is our salvation. Selah. —Psalm 68:19

Your word I have treasured in my heart, That I may not sin against You. —Psalm 119:11

My soul weeps because of grief; strengthen me according to Your word.
—Psalm 119:28

O Lord, my heart is not proud, nor my eyes haughty; Nor do I involve myself in great matters, or in things too difficult for me. —Psalm 131:1

Surely I have composed and quieted my soul; like a weaned child rests against his mother, my soul is like a weaned child within me. —Psalm 131:2

O Lord, You have searched me and known me. You know when I sit down and when I rise up; you understand my thought from afar. You scrutinize my path and my lying down, And are intimately acquainted with all my ways. —Psalm 139:1-3

Trust in the Lord with all your heart and do not lean on your own understanding. In all your ways acknowledge Him, and He will make your paths straight. —Proverbs 3:5-6

There is an appointed time for everything. And there is a time for every event under heaven—A time to give birth and a time to die; A time to plant and a time to uproot what is planted. A time to kill and a time to heal; A time to tear down and a time to build up. —Eccl. 3:1-2

"You are not to say, 'It is a conspiracy!' In regard to all that this people call a conspiracy, and you are not to fear what they fear or be in dread of it. "It is the Lord of hosts whom you should regard as holy. And He shall be your fear, and He shall be your dread. "Then He shall become a sanctuary; But to both the houses of Israel, a stone to strike and a rock to stumble over, And a snare and a trap for the inhabitants of Jerusalem. —Isa. 8:12-14

"The steadfast of mind You will keep in perfect peace, Because he trusts in You. —Isa. 26:3

For thus the Lord God, the Holy One of Israel, has said, "In repentance and rest you will be saved, in quietness and trust is your strength." But you were not willing, —Isa. 30:15

'Do not fear, for I am with you; do not anxiously look about you, for I am your God. I will strengthen you, surely I will help you, surely I will uphold you with My righteous right hand.' —Isa. 41:10

"For I am the Lord your God, who upholds your right hand, who says to you, 'Do not fear, I will help you.' —Isa. 41:13*

"I am the Lord, I have called You in righteousness, I will also hold You by the hand and watch over You, and I will appoint You as a covenant to the people, as a light to the nations, —Isa. 42:6*

But now, thus says the Lord, your Creator, O Jacob, and He who formed you, O Israel, "Do not fear, for I have redeemed you; I have called you by name; you are Mine! "When you pass through the waters, I will be with you; and through the rivers, they will not overflow you. When you walk through the fire, you will not be scorched, Nor will the flame burn you. "For I am the Lord your God, the Holy One of Israel, your Savior; I have given Egypt as your ransom, Cush and Seba in your place. "Since you are precious in My sight, since you are honored and I love you, I will give other men in your place and other peoples in exchange for your life. "Do not fear, for I am with you; I will bring your offspring from the east, and gather you from the west. —Isa. 43:1-5*

"For the mountains may be removed and the hills may shake, but My loving kindness will not be removed from you, and My covenant of peace will not be shaken," Says the Lord who has compassion on you. —Isa. 54:10*

"No weapon that is formed against you will prosper; and every tongue that accuses you in judgment you will condemn. This is the heritage of the servants of the Lord, and their vindication is from Me," declares the Lord. —Isa. 54:17*

The righteous man perishes, and no man takes it to heart; And devout men are taken away, while no one understands. For the righteous man is taken away from evil, He enters into peace; they rest in their beds, Each one who walked in his upright way. —Isa. 57:1-2*

"Blessed is the man who trusts in the Lord and whose trust is the Lord. "For he will be like a tree planted by the water, that extends its roots by a stream and will not fear when the heat comes; but its leaves will be

green, and it will not be anxious in a year of drought nor cease to yield fruit. —Jer. 17:7-8

If it be so, our God whom we serve is able to deliver us from the furnace of blazing fire; and He will deliver us out of your hand, O king. But even if He does not, let it be known to you, O king, that we are not going to serve your gods or worship the golden image that you have set up." —Daniel 3:17-18

Then he said to me, "This is the word of the Lord to Zerubbabel saying, 'Not by might nor by power, but by My Spirit,' says the Lord of hosts. —Zech. 4:6

"Blessed are the poor in spirit, for theirs is the kingdom of heaven. —Matt. 5:3

"Blessed are those who have been persecuted for the sake of righteousness, for theirs is the kingdom of heaven. "Blessed are you when people insult you and persecute you, and falsely say all kinds of evil against you because of Me. Rejoice and be glad, for your reward in heaven is great; for in the same way they persecuted the prophets who were before you. —Matt. 5:10-12

"You are the salt of the earth; but if the salt has become tasteless, how can it be made salty again? It is no longer good for anything, except to be thrown out and trampled under foot by men. "You are the light of the world. A city set on a hill cannot be hidden; nor does anyone light a lamp and put it under a basket, but on the lamp stand, and it gives light to all who are in the house. Let your light shine before men in such a way that they may see your good works, and glorify your Father who is in heaven. —Matt. 5:13-16

"For this reason I say to you, do not be worried about your life, as to what you will eat or what you will drink; nor for your body, as to what you will put on. Is not life more than food, and the body more than clothing? Look at the birds of the air, that they do not sow, nor reap nor gather into barns, and yet your heavenly Father feeds them. Are

you not worth much more than they? And who of you by being worried can add a single hour to his life? "So do not worry about tomorrow; for tomorrow will care for itself. Each day has enough trouble of its own.
—Matt. 6:25-27, 34

And who of you by being worried can add a single hour to his life?
—Matt. 6:27

"Come to Me, all who are weary and heavy-laden, and I will give you rest. Take My yoke upon you and learn from Me, for I am gentle and humble in heart, and you will find rest for your souls. For My yoke is easy and My burden is light." —Matt. 11:28-30

But immediately Jesus spoke to them, saying, "Take courage, it is I; do not be afraid." Peter said to Him, "Lord, if it is You, command me to come to You on the water." And He said, "Come!" And Peter got out of the boat, and walked on the water and came toward Jesus. But seeing the wind, he became frightened, and beginning to sink, he cried out, "Lord, save me!" Immediately Jesus stretched out His hand and took hold of him, and said to him, "You of little faith, why did you doubt?" When they got into the boat, the wind stopped. And those who were in the boat worshiped Him, saying, "You are certainly God's Son!"
—Matt. 14:27-33

Leaving the crowd, they took Him along with them in the boat, just as He was; and other boats were with Him. And there arose a fierce gale of wind, and the waves were breaking over the boat so much that the boat was already filling up. Jesus Himself was in the stern, asleep on the cushion; and they woke Him and said to Him, "Teacher, do You not care that we are perishing?" And He got up and rebuked the wind and said to the sea, "Hush, be still." And the wind died down and it became perfectly calm. And He said to them, "Why are you afraid? Do you still have no faith?" They became very much afraid and said to one another, "Who then is this, that even the wind and the sea obey Him?"
—Mark 4:36-41

For they all saw Him and were terrified. But immediately He spoke with them and said to them,"Take courage; it is I, do not be afraid." 51 Then He got into the boat with them, and the wind stopped; and they were utterly astonished, —Mark 6:50-51

Behold, I have given you authority to tread on serpents and scorpions, and over all the power of the enemy, and nothing will injure you. —Luke 10:19

Indeed, the very hairs of your head are all numbered. Do not fear; you are more valuable than many sparrows. —Luke 12:7

When they bring you before the synagogues and the rulers and the authorities, do not worry about how or what you are to speak in your defense, or what you are to say; for the Holy Spirit will teach you in that very hour what you ought to say." —Luke 12:11-12

"For God so loved the world, that He gave His only begotten Son, that whoever believes in Him shall not perish, but have eternal life. —John 3:16

But an hour is coming, and now is, when the true worshipers will worship the Father in spirit and truth; for such people the Father seeks to be His worshipers. God is spirit, and those who worship Him must worship in spirit and truth." —John 4:23-24

How can you believe, when you receive glory from one another and you do not seek the glory that is from the one and only God? —John 5:44

So Jesus was saying to those Jews who had believed Him, "If you continue in My word, then you are truly disciples of Mine; and you will know the truth, and the truth will make you free." So if the Son makes you free, you will be free indeed. —John 8:31, 32, 36

The thief comes only to steal and kill and destroy; I came that they may have life, and have it abundantly. —John 10:10

Jesus said to her, "I am the resurrection and the life; he who believes in Me will live even if he dies, and everyone who lives and believes in Me will never die. Do you believe this?" —John 11:25-26

"Do not let your heart be troubled; believe in God, believe also in Me. In My Father's house are many dwelling places; if it were not so, I would have told you; for I go to prepare a place for you. If I go and prepare a place for you, I will come again and receive you to Myself, that where I am, there you may be also. 4 And you know the way where I am going." —John 14:1-4

I will ask the Father, and He will give you another Helper, that He may be with you forever; that is the Spirit of truth, whom the world cannot receive, because it does not see Him or know Him, but you know Him because He abides with you and will be in you. —John 14:16-17

He who has My commandments and keeps them is the one who loves Me; and he who loves Me will be loved by My Father, and I will love him and will disclose Myself to him." Jesus answered and said to him, "If anyone loves Me, he will keep My word; and My Father will love him, and We will come to him and make Our abode with him. —John 14:21, 23

Peace I leave with you; My peace I give to you; not as the world gives do I give to you. Do not let your heart be troubled, nor let it be fearful. —John 14:27

Abide in Me, and I in you. As the branch cannot bear fruit of itself unless it abides in the vine, so neither can you unless you abide in Me. I am the vine, you are the branches; he who abides in Me and I in him, he bears much fruit, for apart from Me you can do nothing. If anyone does not abide in Me, he is thrown away as a branch and dries up; and they gather them, and cast them into the fire and they are burned. If you abide in Me, and My words abide in you, ask whatever you wish, and it will be done for you. —John 15:4-7

But I tell you the truth, it is to your advantage that I go away; for if I do not go away, the Helper will not come to you; but if I go, I will send Him to you. —John 16:7

I do not ask You to take them out of the world, but to keep them from the evil one. —John 17:15

But you will receive power when the Holy Spirit has come upon you; and you shall be My witnesses both in Jerusalem, and in all Judea and Samaria, and even to the remotest part of the earth." —Acts 1:8

And hope does not disappoint, because the love of God has been poured out within our hearts through the Holy Spirit who was given to us. —Rom 5:5

But God demonstrates His own love toward us, in that while we were yet sinners, Christ died for us. —Rom 5:8

Therefore there is now no condemnation for those who are in Christ Jesus. For the law of the Spirit of life in Christ Jesus has set you free from the law of sin and of death. —Rom 8:1-2

But if the Spirit of Him who raised Jesus from the dead dwells in you, He who raised Christ Jesus from the dead will also give life to your mortal bodies through His Spirit who dwells in you. —Rom 8:11

For you have not received a spirit of slavery leading to fear again, but you have received a spirit of adoption as sons by which we cry out, "Abba!" "Father!" —Rom 8:15

That the creation itself also will be set free from its slavery to corruption into the freedom of the glory of the children of God. —Rom 8:21

Who will separate us from the love of Christ? Will tribulation, or distress, or persecution, or famine, or nakedness, or peril, or sword? But in all these things we overwhelmingly conquer through Him who loved us. For I am convinced that neither death, nor life, nor angels, nor principalities, nor things present, nor things to come, nor pow-ers, nor height, nor depth, nor any other created thing, will be able to separate us from the love of God, which is in Christ Jesus our Lord. —Rom 8:35, 37-39

For I am convinced that neither death, nor life, nor angels, nor princi-palities, nor things present, nor things to come, nor powers, nor height, nor depth, nor any other created thing, will be able to separate us from the love of God, which is in Christ Jesus our Lord. —Rom 8:38-39

So faith comes from hearing, and hearing by the word of Christ. —Rom 10:17

Therefore I urge you, brethren, by the mercies of God, to present your bodies a living and holy sacrifice, acceptable to God, which is your spiri-tual service of worship. And do not be conformed to this world, but be transformed by the renewing of your mind, so that you may prove what the will of God is, that which is good and acceptable and perfect. —Rom 12:1-2

But he who doubts is condemned if he eats, because his eating is not from faith; and whatever is not from faith is sin. —Rom 14:23

Now may the God of hope fill you with all joy and peace in believ-ing, so that you will abound in hope by the power of the Holy Spirit. —Rom 15:13

The God of peace will soon crush Satan under your feet. The grace of our Lord Jesus be with you. —Rom 16:20

For though we walk in the flesh, we do not war according to the flesh, for the weapons of our warfare are not of the flesh, but divinely powerful for the destruction of fortresses. We are destroying speculations and every lofty thing raised up against the knowledge of God, and we are taking every thought captive to the obedience of Christ, —2 Cor. 10:3-5

It was for freedom that Christ set us free; therefore keep standing firm and do not be subject again to a yoke of slavery. —Gal. 5:1

That the God of our Lord Jesus Christ, the Father of glory, may give to you a spirit of wisdom and of revelation in the knowledge of Him. I pray that the eyes of your heart may be enlightened, so that you will know what is the hope of His calling, what are the riches of the glory of His inheritance in the saints, and what is the surpassing greatness of His power toward us who believe. These are in accordance with the working of the strength of His might —Eph 1:17-19

So that Christ may dwell in your hearts through faith; and that you, being rooted and grounded in love, may be able to comprehend with all the saints what is the breadth and length and height and depth, and to know the love of Christ which surpasses knowledge, that you may be filled up to all the fullness of God. —Eph 3:17-19

So this I say, and affirm together with the Lord, that you walk no longer just as the Gentiles also walk, in the futility of their mind, and that you be renewed in the spirit of your mind, and put on the new self, which in the likeness of God has been created in righteousness and holiness of the truth. —Eph 4:17, 23-24

Do not grieve the Holy Spirit of God, by whom you were sealed for the day of redemption. —Eph 4:30

Finally, be strong in the Lord and in the strength of His might. Put on the full armor of God, so that you will be able to stand firm against the schemes of the devil. For our struggle is not against flesh and blood, but against the rulers, against the powers, against the world forces of this darkness, against the spiritual forces of wickedness in the heavenly places. Therefore, take up the full armor of God, so that you will be able to resist in the evil day, and having done everything, to stand firm. Stand firm therefore, having girded your loins with truth, and having put on the breastplate of righteousness, and having shod your feet with the preparation of the gospel of peace; in addition to all, taking up the shield of faith with which you will be able to extinguish all the flaming arrows of the evil one. And take the helmet of salvation, and the sword of the Spirit, which is the word of God. —Eph 6:10-17

More than that, I count all things to be loss in view of the surpassing value of knowing Christ Jesus my Lord, for whom I have suffered the loss of all things, and count them but rubbish so that I may gain Christ, and may be found in Him, not having a righteousness of my own derived from the Law, but that which is through faith in Christ, the righteousness which comes from God on the basis of faith, that I may know Him and the power of His resurrection and the fellowship of His sufferings, being conformed to His death; in order that I may attain to the resurrection from the dead. Not that I have already obtained it or have already become perfect, but I press on so that I may lay hold of that for which also I was laid hold of by Christ Jesus. —Phil 3:8-12

Be anxious for nothing, but in everything by prayer and supplication with thanksgiving let your requests be made known to God. —Phil 4:6

Finally, brethren, whatever is true, whatever is honorable, whatever is right, whatever is pure, whatever is lovely, whatever is of good repute, if there is any excellence and if anything worthy of praise, dwell on these things. —Phil 4:8

And my God will supply all your needs according to His riches in glory in Christ Jesus. —Phil 4:19

So that you will walk in a manner worthy of the Lord, to please Him in all respects, bearing fruit in every good work and increasing in the knowledge of God; —Colossians 1:10

That is, the mystery which has been hidden from the past ages and generations, but has now been manifested to His saints, to whom God willed to make known what is the riches of the glory of this mystery among the Gentiles, which is Christ in you, the hope of glory. —Colossians 1:26-27

May the Lord direct your hearts into the love of God and into the stead-fastness of Christ. —2 Thess. 3:5

For God has not given us a spirit of timidity, but of power and love and discipline. —2 Tim 1:7

Consider what I say, for the Lord will give you understanding in everything. —2 Tim 2:7

Therefore, since the children share in flesh and blood, He Himself likewise also partook of the same, that through death He might render powerless him who had the power of death, that is, the devil, and might free those who through fear of death were subject to slavery all their lives. —Heb 2:14-15

Now faith is the assurance of things hoped for, the conviction of things not seen. And without faith it is impossible to please Him, for he who comes to God must believe that He is and that He is a rewarder of those who seek Him. —Heb 11:1, 6

And without faith it is impossible to please Him, for he who comes to God must believe that He is and that He is a rewarder of those who seek Him. —Heb 11:6

By faith Abraham, when he was called, obeyed by going out to a place which he was to receive for an inheritance; and he went out, not knowing where he was going. —Heb 11:8

Fixing our eyes on Jesus, the author and perfecter of faith, who for the joy set before Him endured the cross, despising the shame, and has sat down at the right hand of the throne of God. —Heb 12:2

Do not neglect to show hospitality to strangers, for by this some have entertained angels without knowing it. —Heb 13:2

So that we confidently say, "The Lord is my helper, I will not be afraid. What will man do to me?" —Heb 13:6

Therefore humble yourselves under the mighty hand of God, that He may exalt you at the proper time, casting all your anxiety on Him, because He cares for you. —1 Peter 5:6-7

Be of sober spirit, be on the alert. Your adversary, the devil, prowls around like a roaring lion, seeking someone to devour. But resist him, firm in your faith, knowing that the same experiences of suffering are being accomplished by your brethren who are in the world. —1 Peter 5:8-9

Grace and peace be multiplied to you in the knowledge of God and of Jesus our Lord; seeing that His divine power has granted to us everything pertaining to life and godliness, through the true knowledge of Him who called us by His own glory and excellence. —2 Peter 1:2-3

If we say that we have fellowship with Him and yet walk in the darkness, we lie and do not practice the truth; but if we walk in the Light as He Himself is in the Light, we have fellowship with one another, and the blood of Jesus His Son cleanses us from all sin. If we say that we have no sin, we are deceiving ourselves and the truth is not in us. If we confess our sins, He is faithful and righteous to forgive us our sins and to cleanse us from all unrighteousness. —1 John 1:6-9

You are from God, little children, and have overcome them; because greater is He who is in you than he who is in the world. —1 John 4:4

There is no fear in love; but perfect love casts out fear, because fear involves punishment, and the one who fears is not perfected in love. —1 John 4:18

We love, because He first loved us. —1 John 4:19

For whatever is born of God overcomes the world; and this is the victory that has overcome the world—our faith. —1 John 5:4

Behold, I stand at the door and knock; if anyone hears My voice and opens the door, I will come in to him and will dine with him, and he with Me. —Rev. 3:20

But for the cowardly and unbelieving and abominable and murderers and immoral persons and sorcerers and idolaters and all liars, their part will be in the lake that burns with fire and brimstone, which is the second death." —Rev. 21:8

ABOUT RABBI K. A. SCHNEIDER

Messianic Rabbi K. A. Schneider, a Jewish believer in Jesus and end-times messenger of the LORD, delivers the Word of the LORD with true passion of the Holy Spirit. At the age of 20 years old, the LORD appeared to him, supernaturally, as Jesus, the Messiah. He has since pastored, traveled as an evangelist, and served as rabbi of a messianic congregation.

You can watch Rabbi Schneider on television each week on his international television broadcast, "Discovering The Jewish Jesus," which is listed on your TV guide as "The Jewish Jesus." For a list of times and stations that Rabbi Schneider broadcasts in your area, go to www.DiscoveringTheJewishJesus.com and hit the "Ways To Watch" link.

Through understanding the Old Testament and its prophetic nature, with Yeshua as its fulfillment, the viewer's faith is strengthened, increased relationship and intimacy with the LORD is discovered, and an end-times vision of life is crystallized. "Discovering The Jewish Jesus" is an end-times ministry, strengthening the church and calling her to be a readied bride for the return of the Bridegroom, Yeshua Ha Mashiach (Jesus The Messiah).

For more information about Rabbi Schneider
and his international television ministry,
please visit us at:

www.DiscoveringTheJewishJesus.com
www.facebook/Discovering-The-Jewish-Jesus-with-Rabbi-Schneider